Susan E. Burke

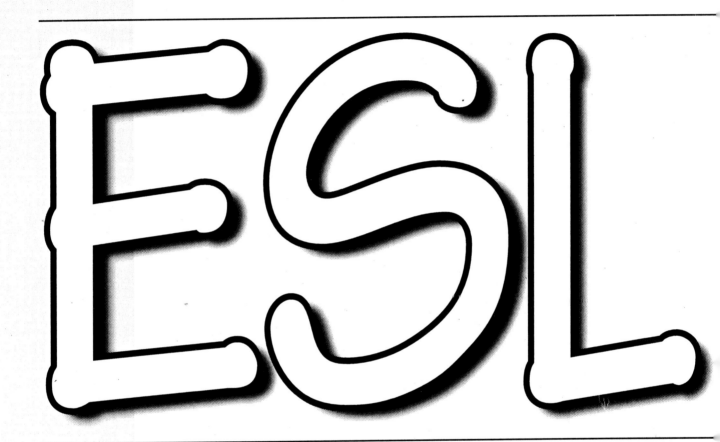

Creating a Quality English as a Second Language Program

A Guide for Churches

FAITH ALIVE®
Christian Resources

Grand Rapids, Michigan

I am grateful to the Keys to English Task Force of the San Jose Presbytery in California for their provision of financial assistance, opportunities for research in local congregations, and ongoing commentary and suggestions. Thanks also goes to numerous members of various congregations who shared their time with me in discussing ESL programming, to First Presbyterian Church of Milpitas, California, for letting me experiment, and to Tom for his continual support.

Faith Alive Christian Resources published by CRC Publications. *Creating a Quality ESL Program,* © 1998 by CRC Publications, 2850 Kalamazoo Ave. SE, Grand Rapids, MI 49560. All rights reserved. With the exception of brief excerpts for review purposes, no part of this book may be reproduced in any manner whatsoever without written permission from the publisher. Printed in the United States of America on recycled paper. ♻
1-800-333-8300

Library of Congress Cataloging-in-Publication Data
Burke, Susan E., 1964-
    Creating a quality ESL program: a guide for churches / Susan E. Burke.
        p.   cm.
    ISBN 1-56212-343-2
    1. English language—Study and teaching—Foreign speakers.
2. English language—Study and teaching—United States.
3. Church and education—United States. I. Title. II. Title: Creating a quality English as a second language program.
PE1128.A2B857   1998
428'.007'073—DC21   98-16037
                                                               CIP

10 9 8 7 6 5 4 3

TABLE OF CONTENTS

CHAPTER 1

Questions People Ask About ESL

Welcome to the world of English as a Second Language! I have personally found teaching ESL to be a rewarding experience at many levels. It's given me opportunities to develop friendships with people from other countries, to share my culture, and to get to know other cultures. Teaching ESL also has given me the opportunity to help learners acquire language skills that are essential for survival in a new country, for career advancement, for educational purposes, and for a host of other reasons.

People generally have a lot of questions about ESL. This is especially true for individuals who are considering starting an ESL program on their church campus or for people who are thinking about teaching ESL as missionaries in foreign countries. On the pages that follow are some of the questions that I am often asked about teaching English as a Second Language. I have also added a few questions of my own for your consideration because I believe that they are relevant to this initial discussion. These questions should give you a general idea of what ESL is and isn't. I want you to know what you and your church/mission organization would or should be dealing with if you decide to become involved in the teaching of ESL.

Who Should Read This Book?

This book is for anyone who is or wishes to be involved in a Christian ESL program at any level. Its purpose is to give people a vision of what an ESL program might look like on their particular church campus or within the context of a specific mission agency. *ESL* is especially written for

volunteer tutors/teachers, ESL coordinators, pastors, church leaders, and missionary agencies who are considering starting an ESL program for adults. It is also aimed at those churches/agencies who already have ESL programs but are looking for more resources and information to train their volunteers, to expand their program, or to experiment with some new ideas. Special attention has been placed upon keeping this volume nontechnical so that it is easily readable and understandable for those who are not professionally trained in ESL methodology.

What Is ESL?

A person from a non-English-speaking country (or ethnic group) speaks his native language as a first language (any language other than English). For example, a person from Japan speaks Japanese as his first language. When this person begins to learn English, it becomes his second language. (Note that if English is being taught in a foreign country, it is sometimes called EFL or English as a Foreign Language.)

Is ESL Education the Same Thing as Bilingual Education?

No, not really. These are two basically different approaches to a person learning another language. The goal of Bilingual education is for a person to become fluent in two languages: the learner's native tongue and a second language, which in this case happens to be English. A Bilingual approach differs from an ESL approach in that instruction often occurs in the learner's first language or in a combination of the first and the second languages.

Perhaps some of you who are native English speakers studied German in high school. If the teacher spoke mainly in English during the class (gave all of the explanations, etc.) and had you repeat German phrases, then that's something like a Bilingual class. In such a class the teacher usually is fluent in the students' first language so that she can teach using that language. Most commonly, Bilingual programs are found in elementary schools, although Bilingual education can be aimed at people of any age.

In pointing to the successes of Bilingual-education programs, proponents often cite the metacognitive (mental flexibility) advantages of being a bilingual individual. They also insist that by preserving a person's first language, you also preserve his individual culture. Languages, after all, contain cultural elements that help to describe concepts distinctive to a particular culture. ESL programs, these people would argue, are potentially destructive of native cultures because they force the learner to integrate into the dominant society and to use the dominant language of that particular country.

Unlike Bilingual programs, ESL programs most often focus on teaching the person one language—English. ESL proponents generally believe that the most direct way to acquire a particular language is to use that language solely. Consequently, classes are conducted in the learner's second, or target, language—the one he hopes to acquire. That doesn't mean students are encouraged to forget their first language; it's assumed that the first language is still spoken outside the classroom with family and friends. But to help speed the learning process, the classroom session itself focuses only on English.

From my observation, the criticism leveled at ESL programs—that its proponents intend to destroy other languages and cultures—is incorrect and unfounded. To the contrary, most ESL instructors I have known over the

past ten years are very interested in their learners' cultures and do a great deal to promote understanding and respect for those cultures in their classrooms.

Practically speaking, what often happens is that ESL instructors and learners are greatly focused on the task at hand—learning English. They believe that acquiring English speaking and writing skills is necessary for a person to survive in an English-speaking society and that without the ability to speak English, it's almost impossible for people to get a job, to get an education, or to be a part of a community. I prefer to think of learning English simply as a skill, like knowing how to use a computer or drive a car. In offering ESL instruction, I am certainly not proposing that an individual forsake his native language or culture. I and others who offer this instruction are simply attempting to help our neighbors survive in a society that is strange to them.

Perhaps some of the philosophical differences between Bilingual educators and ESL educators have developed because of the audiences that each group works with on a regular basis. In teaching English to adults, we are often dealing with individuals who have *immediate* needs to learn English quickly for employment, education, and communication in society. Bilingual educators are often (though certainly not always) dealing with childhood education issues; thus, those programs focus on what is deemed socially, economically, and intellectually best for individuals over a longer period of instructional time (sometimes spanning as much as twelve years).

Unfortunately, many language professionals tend to fall into one camp or the other—drawing the line between themselves in the sand. We would be better served if people, especially in the church, would recognize that there is a place for both ESL and Bilingual language programs. Each program has its advantages and disadvantages. The type of language program that you choose for your church or organization will largely depend upon the end results that you want your learner to obtain.

Obviously, this book focuses on ESL programs; but I've included the basic philosophies of these two language approaches in case you should encounter a discussion on this subject.

Is There Really a Need for Additional ESL Programs?

Depending on where you live, the need could be small or great. Where I live, on the west coast, the need is great!

There are ESL programs throughout Canada and the U.S. and around the world. Many of them are centered in large urban areas where the number of immigrants and internationals tends to be higher. The best way for you to assess the need for an ESL program in your area is to find out what types of people are living in your church neighborhood; that will give you some idea about the population you might be able to reach with this service. You can either do a simple survey yourself or look for information at your local public library. Ask at the information desk for your area's latest demographic records, a good source for information about which ethnic groups live in your area.

If your community has many people from other countries, there are likely to be ESL programs in your area through adult education programs, community colleges, universities, work programs, or private organizations. Many public education programs, though, are currently undergoing severe budget cuts, reducing the number of instructors, administrators, and resources

available to those who are struggling to learn English.

Some corporations are trying to pick up the slack by hiring ESL professionals to provide instruction for their employees. Unfortunately, many businesses are either financially unable or unwilling to provide such instruction over the extended period of time that the learning of a second language requires.

Private language programs are also available. But often the prices charged for these services can be quite high, excluding many individuals who could use the help but are unable to afford it.

As I look at current demographic projections for the next ten years in the U.S., especially in California, I see the number of immigrants and internationals coming to this state rising and the number of educational services offered by the public school system declining. This situation leads me to believe that ESL instruction is going to have to diversify. Other individuals, in addition to ESL professionals, will be needed to meet the demand for language services in the future.

Because of limited resources, government-funded programs in the U.S. cannot be counted on to meet these demands. If the need is to be met, the assistance has to come from somewhere else. And because church members are interested in reaching out to people in the community, the church is a logical place for new programs.

I can personally speak of the need for more ESL programs. When I taught ESL in adult education, we regularly had long waiting lists of individuals wanting to get into a class. Lines of students would pour across the campus on the first day of class, attempting to register for the course.

When I taught at the community college level, I was able to take up to thirty students in my class. However, on the first day of class, I would have anywhere from twenty to sixty extra students in the classroom who wanted to add the class. There were times when I couldn't even physically get into the room because there were so many students. Some of them would beg me to let their daughter or son in the class even if they couldn't get in themselves. A few students got angry, and the dean of the college had to come and escort them out of the classroom. Although that was a rare occurrence, it illustrated the fact that these people realized how much they needed English instruction and how long they would have to wait to get it in a public program.

As an ESL consultant in the private sector, I regularly observed the same trend. When employees were asked whether they were interested in having ESL instruction at their company, the response was an over-whelming yes. But because of financial constraints, the company was often unable to offer instruction to all of those who requested it.

I have often been invited to other countries by ESL program developers and individuals to teach English in public-university and private-program settings. English is viewed as the international business language and the language of choice for most technical fields of study. Individuals in foreign countries view learning English as a positive step toward career advancement.

So the need is there—both in the U.S. and Canada and around the world. It's up to you to assess how great the need might be in your church community—before sinking a lot of time and energy into it. Don't be surprised, though, if, in the course of your investigation, you discover a tremendous need!

To facilitate your investigation, do the following:

- Look at the initial program-assessment questionnaire (pp. 25-29).
- Study your community demographic report. Look specifically for first-generation immigrants, refugees, college students, and business people.
- Use your own firsthand observation of your locale. Interview potential students, coordinators of current ESL programs in your area, teachers, school district officials, heads of training departments in industry, and so on. And good luck!

Do I Have to Know a Lot of Other Languages to Teach ESL?

ESL classes are taught in English. The instructor may or may not speak other languages. It helps if you speak another language just so you can better understand the difficulties your students are going through. It is especially helpful if you know the language of the people you are teaching so that you can better understand the grammatical structures, vocabulary words, pronunciation, or culture of those people. Don't be afraid to proceed, though, if you don't know any other languages, or if it's been many years since you took that high school Spanish class! You can still be a successful teacher of English as a Second Language.

What Qualifications Should a Volunteer Tutor Have to Teach ESL?

You should have a basic knowledge of spoken and written English. I can hear you moaning now: "Well, that counts me out!" Don't worry! If you're a native English speaker, you know more than you think you do, even if that high school grammar class was years ago! You speak English every day. You may not always know the rule governing why we say something a particular way, but you will be able to recognize most errors that your learner makes, just because they will sound strange to you.

The following is a list of personality traits that I believe enhance any instructor's or tutor's success in teaching ESL. *Please don't be intimidated by the length of this list!* You may or may not have all of these traits, but I find this list helpful to think about when asking yourself if teaching ESL is for you.

- You enjoy working with people.
- You feel comfortable working in a one-on-one or small group situation.
- You enjoy sharing knowledge.
- You enjoy getting to know other people and letting them get to know you.
- You can be patient with learners who are struggling with English.
- You can tolerate a little ambiguity. (For example, if you and your learner don't understand each other 100 percent of the time, you can feel okay about it.)
- You like to facilitate instead of control. (You try to help learners do things for themselves instead of doing things for them.)
- You can be a little uninhibited when it comes to acting things out. (Sometimes you find yourself doing crazy things to get your learners to understand!)
- You don't mind scrounging around your house or the community for teaching materials.
- You can be flexible. (You may have to change your plans to meet learners' needs.)
- You are willing to learn new information through training, reading, sharing with other tutors, and having new experiences.
- You have a sense of humor!

Do I Need to Have Training to Teach ESL?

Do you have to be a professional ESL instructor to teach ESL? No, you don't. Many volunteer tutors without a degree in TESOL (Teachers of English to Speakers of Other Languages) have successfully worked with ESL learners at all English levels. Volunteers are very important because they can provide a one-on-one or small group language-learning experience. Many language learners are looking for this kind of individual help but have a difficult time finding it in the public schools and colleges.

I believe that some basic training in ESL is necessary so that you can feel confident about what you're doing and know that your learners are being well served. Believe me, there is nothing worse than standing up in front of a group of students and ad-libbing because you're not really sure of what you're doing!

Will Learners Be Motivated to Study English?

Yes! One of the things that I enjoy most about teaching ESL is that the learners are usually extremely motivated, especially if they have a goal in mind. If they are seeking relationships with other native speakers to fit into society, if they are seeking a job or a promotion, if they want to help their children succeed in school, or if they just want to build up their English skills to feel more confident in social situations, they will more than likely be very motivated.

On the other hand, if they don't feel the need to learn English because they can function in their own ethnic communities without it, if their culture doesn't value traditional education, if they feel they are too old to learn English, if they feel forced to learn English by a parent or an employer, or if they are going to go back to their own country shortly, learners will often be much less motivated to learn.

How successful a learner is in acquiring English often hinges upon how motivated he/she is to learn the language in the first place. Fortunately, the majority of those who seek out ESL services will be very motivated, making learning an enjoyable experience for both you and them.

What Are Some of the Difficulties that We Might Encounter in Starting an ESL Program?

Here is a list of the difficulties that you may encounter, with a brief description of each. I have also included some possible solutions to those difficulties.

Advertising

Unless you have some particular source for supplying learners to your program, you will have to advertise to let learners know that you exist. I would recommend using every advertising resource available to your church, including church newsletters, bulletins, and so on. If the members of your congregation are aware of the program, they can recommend it to their coworkers and neighbors. Perhaps a brief announcement can be made during a church service.

There are also outside advertising means, such as the community sections of newspapers and weekly advertising circulars. Another means of advertising is placing flyers in ethnic markets and restaurants. Leaving flyers at libraries, adult schools, and community colleges can be very successful as well. It may be necessary to obtain permission from authorities at these locations. Look for bulletin boards where you can post your ad at any location.

Word-of-mouth is also a successful way to advertise, and we get a number of our learners this way. If learners feel they're getting the help they need, they'll often bring other family members and friends.

Networking works too. As you get to know other private organizations in your area that are offering ESL classes, sometimes you can help each other by advertising one another's programs. Some program leaders might be afraid to lose learners, but we find that learners often go to a program in their area. Proximity is crucial. And it's important for you to help learners find a program that will work for them, so they'll stick with it! You'll be doing them a favor in the long run by encouraging them to go to the ESL program in their neighborhood.

Another source for advertising might be an ethnic leader, perhaps a pastor, who can refer learners to your program. It would be good to hook up with an ethnic church and let the members know you're offering ESL services.

Most of all, look around your area. If there is some local gathering place where ethnic learners congregate, advertise there!

What about translating advertisements into various languages and putting the ads in ethnic newspapers? I know some churches that have tried this and had minimal success. I asked the learners in my classes what they thought of this idea. Most said that, as a general rule, elderly people read these papers for news about their homeland but that those who would be most likely to need ESL education were trying to read the English newspapers because they want to fit into American society. I recommend trying to think the way the group you're trying to reach thinks. Many see the adult schools, the library, and the local newspaper as sources of information for ESL classes.

Find out where certain ethnic groups advertise to each other. For example, I know of a large Japanese supermarket in our area that is close to a particular church. That supermarket has a bulletin board where many Japanese people advertise items for sale to other Japanese people. That would be an excellent place to put an ad.

One final advertising idea is to create a mailing list of all of those individuals who have visited your program. Even if the person to whom you send the mailing doesn't use the flyer, he will often give it to a friend or family member.

Ultimately, if you think something might work, try it! If it doesn't, you'll know better next time. If your learners are able to speak well enough, ask them for their opinions about what information to put in the ad and where to place it. Many times, they'll take the ads to their favorite places for you. Just make sure that the ad you create isn't too wordy, especially if you're advertising for beginning ESL learners. (See sample ads in chapter 10.)

Finally, if you advertise and don't get any response at first, don't give up! Perhaps you didn't advertise in the best place, or someone tore your ad down, or you offered the class at a time that wasn't convenient for your learners. You may need to do some reassessment and then try again.

Attendance: Open Entry/Open Exit

As you advertise and as learners hear about the program, they'll begin to trickle in, sometimes too slowly for you. They might show up one week, be gone for two weeks, and then come back again. If you have a class or a small group setting, your numbers can fluctuate greatly from week to week.

On the other hand, if you've just done a bit of local advertising, learners may come in a big crowd of, say, ten or more. One week you may have three learners and the next week you might have thirteen! This situation can make you feel a little crazy from week to week in the beginning. What might make matters worse is that church members will often ask, just after you have begun the program, how many learners you have. There will be times when you're not exactly sure yourself!

Sometimes learners will just disappear without notice. You may begin to question if what you're doing is having any effect, or if you're doing it all wrong: "Have they all quit?" "Did I have bad breath last week?" Your mind can run wild with possible reasons for these sudden disappearances (UFOs?), which is why you need two things to keep you going during this time—flexibility and persistence.

While working for the public schools, I participated in several informal studies to determine why learners left particular ESL programs. Often, the problem had less to do with the program itself and more to do with outside concerns such as transportation, child-care, exhaustion from work, family, and so on.

I have also noticed other reasons for lack of attendance: holidays, weather, and time. If the students' country of origin is celebrating a holiday, they probably won't come to class. If it's sunny, your class members might be outside enjoying themselves. If it's rainy, learners may stay home because they did so on rainy days in their country. If your class time is in the evening or on the weekend, they might be too tired to attend class.

You will quickly discover that learners will come and go with the wind, or so it seems. After a while, however, you'll get a core group of individuals who are committed to the process and will be there every week. If you're using individualized tutoring, they may come more often because they will undoubtedly view the one-on-one teaching as valuable instructional time that they don't want to miss.

Some programs offer set registration periods in which individuals may sign up for a class; the class will then be closed until the next registration period. This approach will provide a little more predictability; however, the nature of dealing with possible ESL learners is that they come and go from foreign countries regularly and often not on any set schedule. Just after you close your registration, you may get a slew of individuals who want to join you! At that point you'll have to decide how flexible you want to be. Learners have regularly told me that one of the reasons they stick with our program is because of its flexibility. They know that the door is always open and that we'll do our best to try to squeeze them in. It's a challenge, but we believe it's worth it!

Teacher/Tutor Recruitment

As you might have guessed, I'm suggesting that volunteers from the church act as tutors for those who need English instruction. But how do you as a church get started in this process?

There are two approaches that you can take for initial recruitment of tutors, depending on whether or not you have an ESL professional or a professional educator in your midst. If you do have a professional who is willing to take on the responsibility of acting as the coordinator for the entire program, you're lucky, or shall we say blessed! That person could probably get the program up and running fairly quickly, simply because he or she is familiar with how educational programs are run. This person could also be responsible for recruiting tutors.

Unfortunately, running an ESL program can be a big job. A lot of educators may have too much on their plates already and may not be willing to take on a project such as this. If that's the case, don't give up. Just because you don't have a professional in charge, doesn't mean you can't have a program. It just means you'll have to take a different approach to recruitment and organization.

If you don't have a professional instructor, you will have to find one or two people who are willing to get some basic ESL training and then act as coordinators. (If the title "ESL Coordinators" seems too scary for those who are just starting out, you could call them "Lead Tutors" or something of that nature.) These people will have to take on some of the coordinating duties, such as program administration. (If you are working as one of the only teachers in a smaller program, you may have to put on the coordinator hat yourself.)

I like a team approach best, if that's possible. Then one person doesn't have to bear all of the responsibility and face the possibility that he or she may get burned out. The team of coordinators will then be in charge of recruiting other tutors from the church and helping them get the same training.

Your approach in setting up a program will probably be determined initially by how many of your church members are interested in participating. At first, you will need coordinators who have caught the vision, who will try tutoring, and who will then be willing to pass their vision and experience along to others in your congregation.

There are various ways of getting people interested in tutoring in ESL. You could make a general announcement to your members during your Sunday church service. You could also offer informational meetings to members by general or personal invitation.

We started with a low-commitment approach because we felt that church members would be afraid to commit long term to a project that they weren't sure about. I made a general announcement in the Sunday bulletin, and the pastor verbally reinforced it from the pulpit during worship services. I had a table on the patio outside the church for two or three weeks, where church members could sign up to help with a small group for one Sunday only. They did not have to prepare anything. All they had to do was show up and help. If they enjoyed it, they could sign up for another week. Eventually, a number of people dropped out, but I had a few people who wanted to continue working with the program. These tutors have continued and have gradually taken on more responsibility as their time and interest have permitted.

Be creative in recruiting church members! If you think a specific strategy might appeal to them, try it! Make it as easy as possible for them to become involved. Unfortunately, people are busy and are often unable or unwilling to commit to a project long term. You could put specific time limits on the commitment if it makes it easier for people to become involved. After people do become interested, though, they should be willing to try ESL instruction at least once a week for six months or so. Any less time is unfair both to the tutor, who will put in time to receive training and to gain tutoring experience, and to the learner, who needs enough time to progress sufficiently in his English skills.

Teacher/Tutor Burnout

One of the main reasons that I wrote this manual was to address burnout. As I interviewed members of various congregations who had discontinued their ESL

programs, I asked why each one thought that the program had ended. Unequivocally, the answer I received most often was tutor burnout. From what I have observed, most tutors begin teaching ESL with a great deal of energy and interest, but somewhere along the way that interest dies (especially if there is no one person in charge of the program). Burnout happens quickly when each tutor is operating on his own without the support and valuable knowledge of other tutors.

The main reason for burnout is the feeling of being overwhelmed by learners' needs or by feelings of inadequacy to deal with the challenges that teaching ESL sometimes presents. When tutors feel alone, they are tempted to quit. Unfortunately, this has happened at some churches—even though the learners have wanted to continue instruction. What kind of message does this send to the learner about the church?

It's very important that churches do their work up front (before the program starts) by making an adequate assessment of their tutors' needs, or they will probably end up paying for it in the end with a dying program. Many tutors I spoke with simply did not receive adequate (or any) training before beginning. Most did not have the resources available to them to continue the program for any length of time. Often, quick-training programs will give potential tutors one or two textbooks and a few teaching tips and then throw them into the teaching arena. The problem is that most learners come with more needs than these few books address.

Tutors need *initial* and *ongoing* training. They need to have tests and questionnaires available to them to determine the needs of their learners. They need curriculum lists to know what material is appropriate to teach each learner. They need a variety of materials to meet varying needs of different learners.

13

They need to know how to change materials to better meet their learner's needs. They need methods of evaluation to determine if what they are teaching is making any difference in the learner's life. And they need other tutors to bounce ideas off of or to get new ideas from. Instead of feeling that they are struggling on their own, they need to feel that they are part of a team.

At our church we have a biweekly ESL team meeting. We discuss upcoming church events, problems any tutor or the ESL program might be having, and further ESL training and techniques. We encourage each other and pray for each other and our students. God has used our time together to meld us into a unified team. I am very fortunate to work with a great group of highly committed people!

I have personally observed tutors running several successful ESL programs. What all of these programs had in common were the qualities I listed above. Along with these, it would be great to have some type of recognition system for the volunteer tutors (by the church, the learners, and the coordinators) so that they know they are appreciated and consequently will feel that they want to continue.

Preexisting Program Regulations

If you are attempting to work within an already existing ESL program, you may or may not have the flexibility that you desire to implement new ideas. You will have to evaluate your situation and determine how you want to apply the information in this book to your particular teaching circumstance.

Here's one possible application (although I am sure there are many others). If you have been sent by a Christian mission organization to teach English and to share your faith within a non-Christian organization,

such as a public university in a foreign country, you will need to exercise caution and use discretion in terms of sharing your Christian beliefs with students during actual work hours. You will want to be sure that you offer quality secular ESL instruction so that you deliver the product that you have promised to the institution. Doing so will help you to gain credibility with the institution and with your learners. You can then begin to pray for opportunities to share your faith in ways appropriate to the institution that you are working for.

Why Should the Church Offer ESL Programs?

Just as there are many different kinds of churches and Christian agencies, so there are many different views on why these organizations should offer ESL programs. As I have examined ESL programs at churches and in denominations, I have observed that all programs had one thing in common: supporters believed that churches should offer English instruction to members of the community because it is necessary and helpful.

Some churches had additional reasons for offering ESL programs. Here are a few:

- The church offered ESL to get people from the community involved in the church; their hope was that later some of these people would become full members.
- ESL was offered as one of many support services provided for refugee families.
- The church used its ESL program as a service project that church members can do in their local community.
- ESL was used as a local mission project offering educational services.
- ESL instruction was made available because of growing needs in a biethnic congregation.
- ESL instruction was used as a means to befriend international college students.

✗ The church offered ESL because of underlying feelings of guilt that church members should be doing something for ethnic groups in the community.

- ESL instruction was used as one way to share the good news of Jesus Christ.

What do you think? Besides helping individuals in the community, are there any other reasons for offering ESL instruction on your church campus? How do you decide which reasons are appropriate?

Some of the reasons listed above are noble and/or practical, and there's nothing wrong with that, but there should be one all-important, primary reason that churches offer ESL programs on their campuses. All other reasons should be secondary.

The church should work with ESL learners because we, as its members, care about people as individuals and want to help them meet their felt needs.

Before we take a closer look at that primary reason, let me briefly address the guilt issue. If any of you feel the need to have an ESL program at your church out of guilt for things that you should be doing for internationals or ethnic populations, then please don't consider it. This book was not written as one more way to pressure you into what you should do. If you are attempting to serve ESL learners out of compulsion, they will figure that out very quickly. God would rather have us give to him and these individuals cheerfully!

I would love to dispel many of the guilt feelings I observe in Christians who are honestly seeking to serve internationals in their community. Many Christians don't have an understanding of what they are up against. They think that if they just try harder or care more, they will succeed in bringing individuals of different language groups and cultures together into their church. They falsely think that they can meet the diverse needs of internationals by just giving more and being less selfish. They haven't considered that these are hard jobs and that loving feelings are not the only tools needed in this endeavor.

Think of this: God totally destroyed communication at the Tower of Babel. I had no idea how messy languages were until I began to study linguistics and saw firsthand how God made well-ordered, yet highly complicated language structures that have taken linguists years to unravel. God made it hard for us to communicate with each other on purpose, and he did an excellent job!

Isn't it amazing that God now seems to be using the very thing that once separated people—language—to pull us back together again? Many churches are now using the teaching of a common language, English, as a tool to reach out to their communities. Only very recently have we begun to gain the tools (more effective teaching techniques, methods, and technology) to reach out in this way to people who are different than ourselves. I have observed church members berating themselves because they haven't done enough for their community. This is my advice to them: "Stop beating yourself up. You haven't had the tools or the training to meet the needs of those in your community. How can you have done in the past what you didn't know how to do until now?"

Please understand, I am not saying that the teaching of ESL is the cure-all for every sociocultural ill. See the teaching of ESL for what it is (a tool that can be used as a bridge out to the community) and not for what it isn't (a way to ease church "should" guilt).

As I said, the primary reason why Christians should work with ESL learners is because we care about these people as individuals, and we want to help them meet their felt needs.

What is a felt need? It's a desire that a learner expresses as being particularly important to him or her. For example, when Jairus fell at the feet of Jesus in Luke 8:41-42, his felt need was that Jesus would come to his house and heal his dying daughter. Obviously, this need was singly important to Jairus. What did Jesus do? He went to Jairus's house and healed his daughter. Jesus listened to the need expressed and then offered his divine assistance to meet that need. This is a pattern repeated over and over in the gospels: Jesus saw needs, and he met them.

How does this relate to ESL instruction? I have observed that learners usually come to me expressing specific needs. I know that I cannot meet a learner's every need, nor do I believe that I am called to do so. What I want to do is meet the greatest needs that an individual expresses and that I feel I am equipped to handle.

A few years ago, I conducted an ethnographic study at a large adult school in the Los Angeles area to determine what learners felt their greatest needs were. I interviewed individuals and compiled their answers. During this investigation I discovered three felt needs that I have heard learners express again and again over the years. The first two are *the need for resources to learn English* and *the need for a sense of community*. (I will discuss learners' third felt need later.)

In terms of resources, learners felt crammed into classrooms. They lacked enough classroom materials. They had a hard time getting parking spaces, and they could not get personal time with the course instructor. Learners also had a hard time getting into the class itself, and many had spent months on a waiting list before being allowed in.

In terms of the need for community, many learners had come from much more interdependent societies. They were used to having immediate and extended family members in close proximity. Community events drew them together regularly with friends, family, neighbors, and business associates.

Upon coming to the U.S., their families were often split up, and they were introduced to a new attitude of independence. Many of these people didn't even know who their neighbors were. Their bosses in this country didn't act as father figures who were looking out for their well-being. Many found themselves living alone, with the television as their only dinner companion.

At the time this study was conducted, these learners expressed a desire for social activities at the school so that they could meet people and make friends. Unfortunately, this didn't happen because of the way that school systems here are normally structured. I found that the North American way of life produced in these immigrants a great deal of culture shock, homesickness, and a longing for the companionship of family and friends.

Throughout eleven years of teaching ESL, I have also observed a third felt need—*the need for spiritual information and/or information about Christianity*. In classroom situations in the public school system and in my work in the private sector, I have often been asked for my opinion or my advice on spiritual matters.

It should not be surprising that I have also been asked many questions about Christianity in English classes at the church. Learners who come specifically to the church for English instruction (instead of some other institution) are often interested in spiritual matters. They assume that the church is a place where they can get some of their questions answered.

ESL learners are interested in what Americans think, and many view Christianity as American in nature, especially if Christianity is not a major part of their native culture. Many learners are interested in reading the Bible because they believe that this is where Americans get a lot of their ideas for government, holidays, cultural standards, and so on. Some have also been interested in Christianity because they are confused by their own religion's many rules and contradictions, and they believe that Christianity has a simple message they can understand. Still others have personal problems that they are seeking to resolve, and they believe that Christianity may offer them some hope.

ESL learners may well have many other needs, but these three—resources, community, and spiritual information—are what I have observed as their most significant felt needs. When I worked in the public school system as well as in the private sector, I could see the needs, but I could do very little about them. I could not offer classroom resources that I did not have. I couldn't socially involve myself with learners because it was frowned upon by administrators. I was under stress professionally about discussing any element of Christianity or spirituality, even when the question had been totally initiated by the learner.

I now know that there is hope for a different kind of ESL program that does what learners want it to do. The church can offer a program that ministers to learners by meeting their expressed felt needs. Members of individual congregations can be equipped to offer resources that will help them learn English. The church already has a built-in sense of community; it is a safe place in

society where individuals can go for spiritual information.

My purpose is not to blame the public school system or private-sector programs. I don't believe that churches should attempt to replace these programs either. Each ESL program serves a certain purpose. But these types of ESL programs, by their very nature, are not set up to meet the personal felt needs of individuals. Only the church, made up of individual Christians, can do that.

Because of that fact, I have developed an ESL program model that offers learners three types of assistance to address their three expressed felt needs.

The first type of assistance addresses the need for resources to learn English. Learners can receive high-quality English instruction, use a variety of materials, and receive personalized assistance at a church campus that is close to their homes. By offering these resources, churches show love to an individual, with the hope that real learning takes place so that he is truly helped in his everyday English needs.

The second type of assistance addresses the need for community. Learners can participate in social and service activities that provide that sense of community. These activities could also lead to a greater integration into the larger church family if the learner chooses to become involved. The church can show the individual that she is loved and cared for and that she belongs.

The third type of assistance addresses the need for spiritual information in response to the many questions that ESL learners have. The church can provide a safe and loving place for them to ask their questions without feeling pushed. Church members can teach learners the Bible, using language and cultural concepts that they can relate to. The church will also encourage learners to make up their own minds about how they choose to apply this information to their lives.

Often in outreach ministries we have the best of intentions; however, we don't end up meeting the needs of our target audience because we're focused on what we want to happen to them through the ministry. My purpose is not to condemn but to suggest that a redirection of focus may be in order for some current church ESL programs. We need to take the focus off of ourselves and what we hope to gain by our efforts.

In seeking to answer the original question of whether there are other reasons for offering ESL on our church campuses, I suggest that we take a hard look at our own motives. I realize that it is hard to let go of what we want to happen in the lives of our learners and in the life of our church, and I want you to know that I am challenging myself with this fact as much as I am challenging you.

In Mark 9:35, Jesus challenges us to be great by being servants of all. Part of that serving process is to listen to those he has called us to help and to meet their expressed needs as best we can. Only through the empowerment of the Holy Spirit, through prayer, and through complete reliance on the Lord are we able to serve these individuals and then entrust them to God and trust his will for their lives.

Perhaps instead of asking, "Why should the church offer ESL programs?" a better question might be "How can the church serve individuals through ESL programs?"

Is It Really Possible for ESL Learners to Become Practicing Christians and to Integrate into an English-Speaking Church?

My answer to this question is a resounding yes! We're very excited about what God has

been doing in our church in terms of bringing ESL learners into a relationship with God. We have a number of ESL learners who have prayed to receive the Lord, have been baptized, and have become members of our church. These learners are currently being discipled and attending worship services.

We encourage learners to get involved in the church as much as possible. ESL learners have regularly attended the church's newcomer's lunch, the annual church picnic, music concerts, and the church's annual women's retreat. When ESL learners take the church membership class, they have a chance to meet and develop relationships with other new members (who are often native English speakers), because part of the class time is spent in small group discussion.

A few learners have started doing small ministry tasks within the church. We have had some learners working as teachers' aides for the children's church school classes. Some have worked as greeters in our hospitality ministry. Others have served food and run games at the church's Fall Family Festival. One man has been working with others in the church doing the gardening for the church grounds. Still others have given their testimonies to the seekers in the ESL classes.

As these new Christians become more mature Christians and as their level of English speaking permits, we encourage them to get into leadership positions within the ESL ministry or into any other ministry that they feel God is calling them to participate in.

It has taken time for this spiritual growth and integration to occur. This is not a fly-by-night ministry, which you can do for a short amount of time and expect to see great results. On the other hand, if you are patient and keep providing opportunities for ESL

Felt Needs ESL Program Model

Upon his entry into and throughout the program the learner chooses
- which type of assistance he wants to accept and when.
- what his results will be for each category.

Type of Assistance Offered	Secular ESL Instruction	Social Activities	Christian ESL Instruction
Learner's Felt Need	Resources to Learn English	Sense of Community	Spiritual Information
Church Member's Role	Serve Learner	Serve Learner	Serve Learner
	Follow God's Word	Follow God's Word	Follow God's Word
God's Word	Love your neighbor as yourself. Matt. 22:39	Love your neighbor as yourself. Matt. 22:39	Therefore go and make disciples of all nations . . . teaching them to obey everything I have commanded you. Matt. 28:19-20
Possible Results, Dependent upon Learner's Choices Throughout the Program	Improved written and spoken English skills	New friends Integration into the family of God in a local congregation	Personal problems resolved Deepened spiritual relationship with God

learners to grow spiritually and to meet and become friends with native speakers in your congregation, integration can happen. We have seen the greatest success in terms of spiritual growth and integration with ESL learners who are intermediate and advanced-level English speakers. Beginners are tough! Still, we work with beginners because they need our help.

The most exciting element of this ministry is how God has used it to change individual learner's lives spiritually. The following are short testimonies that were given by two of our learners when they were baptized. (We helped them write what they wanted to say.) The first woman was an advanced learner, and she gave her testimony in front of the congregation by herself. The second was a low-intermediate learner, and she wanted me to speak along with her.

Teresa

Hi. I'm Teresa Lee. I'm from Taiwan.

About eight months ago, I began searching for meaning in my life after a difficult time when someone had hurt me. I saw a Christian program on TV and prayed, "If there is a God up there, help me!" Later, I began looking for an English class, and I came to this church. I met Susan, and we studied English from the Bible. Through my studies I learned that Jesus offered me forgiveness, and he taught me how to forgive the person who had hurt me. I decided to pray and received the Lord five weeks ago.

I'm happy that Jesus has changed my life.

Choi

Hi. I'm Choi Fan. I'm from Hong Kong. I'm happy to be a Christian, and I love Jesus.

Susan

Choi told me that she grew up learning Buddhism from her mother. When she grew older, she asked questions about Buddhism of her mother, other family members, and friends, but each person always gave her a different answer.

She found Buddhism to be a very confusing religion.

Choi came to this church eighteen months ago when she started studying English here.

When she studied the Bible, she began to feel happy. She felt in her heart that what Jesus said was true.

She wanted to follow what Jesus said, so she prayed to receive him into her heart in May of this past year.

CHAPTER 2

Keys to a Successful ESL Program

If you read chapter 1, you have a feeling for what ESL is and isn't. I hope the first chapter has generated some interest for you and you're wondering what the next step is. What would your church need to do to start an English as a Second Language program on its campus?

Most successful secular ESL programs have several key elements that contribute to their longevity; they are as follows:

- Assessment—Find out who your learners will be and what resources you have.
- Training—Obtain training for your tutors.
- Testing—Determine the English levels of your learners.
- Curriculum/Materials—Figure out what to teach learners and acquire instructional materials.
- Evaluation—Ask your learners and tutors if needs are being met.
- Customization—Change your program to meet individual learner needs.

I have taken these key elements for a successful program and placed them into a list that can be followed step-by-step by church members in order to begin creating an ESL program at their particular location.

- Assess your community.
- Evaluate your church's resources.
- Rally internal support.
- Decide how resources will be obtained and get them.
- Train tutors.
- Implement program.
- Evaluate program.
- Change program to meet needs based upon evaluation.
- Inform supporters.

This list is not static; once you complete it, you're not finished. It is a dynamic list, because even after the program has begun, you will still need to gain more resources, get more training for your tutors, and continue evaluating and changing to meet your learners' needs. Even with these basic elements, you can and should continue to improve on each of the items in this list. That will really make your program successful.

Some people have asked me if it is necessary to have all of these elements in a program—"Aren't there any short cuts?" Unfortunately, there aren't any that I know of. I have observed (in researching various ESL programs in existence, or more likely *not* in existence) that if a program does not have these components, it will not last. Many churches have started programs with almost no training or materials available to their tutors, and six months later the tutors burned out.

I recommend going step-by-step and making sure that each program element is in place. You will need to pay with your time in the beginning. In the six months prior to the start-up of the ESL program on our campus, my pastor took a lot of pressure off me by saying, "It may take us a while to get there, but at least we're headed in the right direction." That has proved to be true. So allow yourselves the time it takes to get these key elements in place. You'll save yourselves a lot of headaches in the long run.

Assess Your Community

Okay, let's get started. The first step in deciding if an ESL program will work for your church is assessing your community. The community surrounding each church is different, so you can't necessarily judge what you might do by what another church is doing across town. You should look at what's best for your congregation and your locale.

Some churches have had demographic reports done by private agencies at various radiuses around their churches to determine ethnic breakdown. If such a service is not available to you for financial or other reasons, go to your closest public library and ask for the demographic report for your city or area. From it you can learn a great deal about the people who live in your community and how you might best help them.

Obviously, you will be looking for what specific ethnic groups are in your area, but you can also glean a lot of other information about these groups and begin to make guesses about what your program might look like. For example, if your report says that there are a large number of people of a particular ethnic group who are employed by manufacturers, then you can begin to make some guesses about their work hours.

You can use this information to determine what times would be best suited for offering an ESL class. For example, you would know that it would be foolish to offer classes from 10:00 a.m. to 12:00 p.m. Monday through Friday if the people you are trying to serve work from 9:00 a.m. to 5:00 p.m. every day.

After you have demographic information, observe. Look around and see if what you've read seems to fit your locale. If you have the opportunity, ask a few of the people that you see in your area about their interest in and time preference for an ESL class. Speak with ethnic coworkers at your place of employment. Visit an ethnic restaurant or store or your local library to make contacts.

You will get different answers depending on who you talk to. A morning class might be fine for a Japanese housewife, but a working Hispanic male might want classes on weekends or in the evenings. You might decide that you're going to aim for the largest target group in your area first. Use any connections that you have to start talking to ethnic groups about their needs. At first you may feel a bit awkward, but eventually you'll begin to get a sense of the needs in your community.

Perhaps you already have a group of people you think you would like to work with—for example, the parents of children that your church serves through daycare. But be careful not to assume anything with a group like that. Make sure you interview some of these parents and find out if there is a genuine interest and need for your services. Just because you have targeted a particular group doesn't mean that they will automatically choose you. Find out what they want and need. (I say this from experience.)

You may find a great deal of interest in your services. And in that case, a ready-made population is a wonderful place to start. It could save you from some of the hassles of initial advertising. But don't assume anything. Make sure you ask questions of the people you seek to serve.

Evaluate Your Resources

The next step in deciding if an ESL program will work for you is to evaluate your resources. By looking at the demographics and observing and interviewing a few people, you should begin to get an idea of who you might be working with and what their needs are in terms of time and interest. Armed with this information, you can then determine if you have the resources to meet those needs.

First, ask yourself these questions: Do you have a location where tutors and learners could meet? Do you have people in the church who would be willing to receive some training and then tutor learners? Do you have money to buy materials for the learners, or will this be a self-supporting program in which learners will pay a fee? If you don't want an ongoing program, are you willing to put in the time to get the program up and running and then maintain it for at least six months to a year? (In chapter 3, I have included a program assessment questionnaire for a more complete appraisal of your resources.)

Rally Internal Support

Next, you will need to rally internal support. Church members need to know what you're thinking and where you would like to go with your idea. They need a glimpse of the vision so they can get behind you and support you prayerfully, sacrificially, and financially. By sacrificially, I mean putting up with all of the little annoyances that are bound to come up as a new program is being implemented (sharing rooms, having extra children in the church school classes or nursery, getting access to copy machines and office supplies, etc.). These things don't have to be a problem if you anticipate problems ahead of time and have a plan of action to deal with them.

You can inform members by speaking in church, placing articles in your church newsletter, attending committee meetings, and communicating with key leaders in your church. You will need this support so that you won't feel alone and overwhelmed. You and perhaps a few others will be acting in the role of educators as you seek to help members understand the basics about language-learning processes and language programs.

Decide Which Resources You'll Use

No program can run without resources. You'll need books and tables and chairs at the very least, and perhaps a whole lot more. You should look at what you already have and what you can obtain through direct purchase or donations. Sometimes church committees have funds that they are willing to share with you. There might be individuals in your congregation who will take a special interest in an ESL program and contribute financially. In many cases the program will need to be self-supporting, requiring learners to pay for everything. Another option is to have learners pay for materials while the church pays for any administrative costs, such as copying, advertising, and mailings.

At our church we have had learners pay for textbooks and classroom copies. The instruction and administrative costs are free. Other church programs I have observed have received donated classroom materials from educational institutions, and the program is entirely free to the learner. Another program at a local church charged the learner a flat fee of $50.00 per ten-week session. Part of this fee was used for materials, and the rest went into a savings account. That church felt it would be fair to eventually hire a professional ESL instructor to teach in the program. (Their current instructor is an ESL professional who is running the program voluntarily.) When their savings account reaches a point that can cover an agreed-upon salary, a paid position will be put into place. As you assess your resources, you will have to see what strategy works for your church and your learners.

Options for Funds

Train Tutors

The next step is training. This is an essential step if you want to avoid tutor burnout, which I talked about in chapter 1. To get started, have tutors read training materials, such as this book, in order to get an overall picture of ESL. By no means have I made a complete list of the many training resources that are currently available for ESL instruction, but I hope the resources in this book will be a jumping-off point for you. You can attend training sessions at other locations, or you can have your own in-house discussions. Just make sure that you don't skip this step!

Implement Programs

After training comes the actual implementation of the program. You will have to assess learners to discover their interests, test them to discover their mastery level of English, assign them appropriate materials, and finally teach them English using a classroom, small group or lab setting, or individual tutoring.

Evaluate Program

The final step is evaluation. Every good educational program has some type of evaluation process to determine if learning has taken place. This process can occur at the end of a course or at a midpoint to determine if in fact the needs that were stated in the beginning of the class are actually being met. Both learners and tutors should be surveyed to get an accurate picture of what learning is taking place. Chapter 7 contains more information on evaluation procedures.

Make Needed Changes

Based upon the results of your evaluation process, you will probably find that some things have been successful while others need to be changed. Don't be afraid to change something if it's not working. Nothing you do has to be set in stone. Some of the most successful programs I have observed are those that have been

evaluated, found faulty in some areas, and changed. There is no sin in experimenting with an idea and then finding out that it doesn't work.

Each ESL program in each church is going to be a little different, depending on who the learners are and what needs they have. You may have to change small things as your learners' situations change. For example, your meeting time may have to change if your learners' work schedules suddenly change. If it's possible, you should try to develop a program that is flexible and grows with your learners.

By the way, my discussion here has been about change, but if there is something your learners really like or seem particularly interested in, by all means keep it! Explore it! Do it! Satisfied "customers" keep coming back.

Inform Supporters

Finally, remember to keep supporters informed about what is happening in your ESL program. Such information will give them a sense of ownership and interest in the program, and it will provide accountability for you and the other tutors. With open lines of communication, you will also be able to verbalize your needs as they arise.

I suggest letting supporters come and visit during class times, inviting them to social activities and parties, writing written reports for them about program process, and assisting learners in writing them thank-you notes and letters. Such gestures are greatly appreciated by supporters.

Now that you've seen the basic recipe, let's look in more depth at each ingredient of a successful ESL program.

CHAPTER 3

Assessing Your Resources

Initial assessment is essential for a successful ESL program. It may be tempting at first to jump in with the teaching aspects of the program and to start dealing with your learners, but this is a plan for failure at one level or another. You must know who and what you're dealing with if you want to adequately meet the needs of your learners. You'll also save yourself a lot of hassles down the trail if you follow the assessment procedures.

It may seem laborious at times to be gathering all of this information, but don't be in such a rush that you don't take the time to set down the building blocks of a solid program. If there is a need in your community for ESL services today, the same need will probably be there the next day and the next.

To assist you in your assessment process, I have developed the following questionnaire. It is simply a tool to get you thinking. You probably won't have all of the answers to all of the questions. Your goal should be to use this tool to see where you need more information and then try to find it.

You can use the questionnaire in a number of different ways. For example, it may be useful as a means to gain information about a group you already have some contact with, such as the parents of children in your church's daycare program. You can also use it to find out what you know about ESL learners in your community and as a guide during your demographic search. In both the former and the latter cases you would be using the questionnaire in a forecasting sense—because you don't know everything about your learners, you are attempting to get a picture of what your program might look like.

The questionnaire will also be useful if you currently have an ESL program at your church but are seeking to improve it. Perhaps some areas of your program need to be explored further. Or you may want to analyze whether you have some of the key elements for a successful program in place. If you have had an ESL program in your church that died out, you may want to use this questionnaire to analyze what went wrong so that you don't duplicate those problems again in your new program. (In this case, word all of the questions in the past tense.)

You should at least have an initial assessment before your program gets started. I do suggest ongoing assessments as well, just to make sure that your program is remaining current with the trends represented in your community.

Program Assessment Questionnaire

This questionnaire is for churches who plan to offer, currently offer, or in the past have offered an ESL program on their campuses. Please answer the following questions to the best of your ability and according to your particular situation.

General Information About Learners
1. Do you have any demographic reports for your community?

2. What is the ethnic makeup of your learners?

3. What are their native languages?

4. What is the educational level of your learners here, or what was it in their country of origin?

5. Have the learners studied English before coming to your class? If so, where?

6. What did the learners study in those classes (reading, writing, grammar, speaking, pronunciation, etc.)?

7. How long have the learners been in the United States or Canada?

8. What is their motivation for coming to the U.S. or Canada (refugee, education, job, better life)?

9. What are the learners' motivations for learning English (help their children, get a better job, make friends, etc.)?

10. Have the learners brought you any examples from their daily lives that illustrate their specific English problems (bills, forms to fill out, problems on the phone, job manuals to read, letters from their child's teacher, etc.)?

11. What are the learners' future goals (job promotion, further education, start own business, etc.)?

Spiritual Information About Learners

1. Have the learners ever been in a church before? If yes, what kind? Where? For how long? Doing what? If no, why not?

2. Do the learners have positive or negative assumptions about the church? What are their assumptions? Why is this so?

3. Do the learners seem to be open to spiritual information? Will they willingly study the Bible or Christian materials?

4. Are the learners currently participating in another church and/or religion? What do you know about those organizations?

5. Why are the learners coming to the church—for secular English instruction, for a sense of community, for spiritual information, for a combination of these, or all of these?

6. How would you categorize your learners in terms of spiritual interest:

   - distracted because they are busy achieving their own goals for work, family, money, etc.?
   - uninterested because they believe that Christianity is not relevant for real life?
   - uninformed because they believe that Christianity teaches the same information that all religions teach (love everyone, be good to everyone, etc.)?
   - hostile to Christianity because they've had a bad experience with it or another religion?
   - fearful because their culture doesn't accept Christianity or their family doesn't want them exposed to Christianity?
   - curious about Christianity because they know very little about it?
   - interested because they've had a good experience with other Christians or the church before?
   - hopeful because they have a problem in their life that their own native religion can't solve, and they hope that Christianity can offer them some answers?
   - wanting to learn because they believe that Christianity is part of American culture, and they want to understand American thinking?
   - seeking real-life answers to some of life's difficult questions?

7. Is the learner a Christian? Has he prayed to receive Christ? Has he been baptized?

8. Does the learner believe that she is a Christian, but you're not sure because of some of the strange or missing information related to her conversion? (Watch out for cults and churches in other countries that teach only part of the gospel message.)

9. Do you have a plan ready for learners who desire to be Christians and want to be baptized and become members of your church? Do you have a plan for their continued growth?

Curriculum

1. Do you plan to use any kind of method, technique, or special program to teach English to your learners? If so, what is it (communicative method, total physical response, natural approach, audio-lingual method, bilingual materials, etc.)?

2. How will you test your learners to determine their English level? What test will be used (CASAS, JOHN Test, TABE, ABLE, BEST, a test made up by you or your program coordinator, a test that accompanied your other materials, a test from this manual)?

3. Is a copy of the test you chose readily available for use? Does it require additional training for individuals to administer?

4. How will the given materials be assigned to learners?

5. What skills will you focus on in your tutoring sessions (reading, writing, listening, speaking, grammar, pronunciation, life skills, American

culture, other)? Have learners expressed a preference?

6. Does it seem like your learners are struggling with one language skill (reading, writing, listening, speaking) more that others, based upon your interviews with them? If they are struggling with one of the skills, what is it? Do you have any idea why this is so (past educational training, learner personality, culture, etc.)?

7. Is a copy of your materials readily available? What will your process be for ordering them? Is any additional training needed in order to use the materials properly? What is the cost of the materials?

8. After examining (or using) the materials, what do you like about them?

9. What do you not like about these materials, and/or how could they be improved?

10. Did the learners seem to enjoy these materials? Why or why not? (This question is for those who have used some ESL materials already.)

11. Do the textbooks have any accompanying resource materials, such as audio- or videotapes, flash or picture cards, games, puzzles, teachers' manuals? Will you use them? Were they helpful? (This question is for those who have used the resource materials already.)

12. Where did you hear about these materials? Do you know of any other places that you could receive ESL materials from?

13. Will you use Christian ESL materials, or will you use a combination of Christian and secular ones? (Explain your choice.)

Based upon your interviews with them, have learners requested or expressed an interest in Christian ESL materials?

14. Who will pay for the materials, photo-copying, etc.? The learners? The church?

Training

1. Do you feel adequately prepared to work with your learners? If yes, why? If no, why not?

2. What do you wish that someone would teach you before you start working with your learners?

3. What do you hope to learn throughout the teaching process about ESL learners? About yourself? About the materials? About teaching?

4. If you were to be offered some secular training today, what would you be interested in learning about (how to set up a lesson plan, how to assess the English level of your learner, how to choose a good textbook, fun activities to do with your learner, basic philosophies and techniques for teaching English, etc.)?

5. If you were to be offered some Christian training today, what would you be interested in learning about (how to share your faith in a culturally sensitive way, how to offer Christian information to non-Christians, how to run a small group for ESL seekers and/or believers, etc.)?

Recruitment

1. Where will your learners come from (church, community, other)?

2. Will you advertise for learners in the community?

3. If you have advertised, what form did you use (flyers, word-of-mouth between learners, orientation meeting, personal invitation, newspaper, radio, TV, other)?

4. What form of advertising was most successful?

5. Where will your tutors come from (church, community, other)?

6. What form of advertising will be used to recruit tutors (personal invitation, general announcement in church bulletin or newsletter, orientation meeting for those interested, other)?

7. Have you ever used brochures, flyers, videos, etc., to advertise your program?

8. Is a copy of your brochure/flyer readily available, or does it need to be developed?

Type of Program

1. Do you want a traditional classroom setting, a small group setting, a language laboratory, or individual tutoring?

2. Based upon your choice in question 1, what will your class size be? How many tutors will you require? What time will you meet? How often will you meet per week?

3. Do you have a room(s), chalkboards, overheads, etc.?

4. Depending upon your program choice, how and where will volunteer tutors be trained for this program?

5. Will you offer daycare for your learners' children?

Evaluation

This evaluation is for those who currently have or have had an ESL program.

1. What did you think were some of the most successful parts of your program? Why were they successful?

2. What parts of your program need improvement?

3. Have teachers/tutors ever filled out an evaluation form or survey about your program? Do you need to develop one?

4. Have learners ever filled out an evaluation form or survey or taken part in an oral evaluation about your program? Do you need to develop a survey?

5. Do you remember anything specific that your learners asked for during the program ("I want to learn more," "Could you teach me about . . .")?

6. Is there anything specific that you would like to know from your learners that might be included on an evaluation form?

7. Have learners continued in or repeated portions of your program? Why or why not?

Roles in an ESL Program: Possible Positions and Associated Duties

In your initial assessment discussion, you must consider one of the most important resources of your ESL program—people. The members of your congregation or the individuals who will serve ESL learners from your organization can fulfill many roles in an ESL program. They are definitely an integral part of any program since so much of what they do is relational. You will need to assess what kind of assistance you are going to get from individuals in your congregation and how long these people are willing to be committed to the program.

I have made a wish list of possible positions and their associated duties that might be covered by individuals from your congregation. If you can't fill all of these positions, the program is still possible. It simply means that one or more individuals have to take on more responsibilities. That is possible, but I do caution against burnout. I think a team approach is a much better response. Still, you have to be realistic and deal with the actual number of people who are willing to help.

If you can't get all of the people on this list, and/or those who are running the program are getting burned out, that's a sign that you'll need to put some limitations on the program. Perhaps you will have to limit the number of participants entering it, or you will have to limit its scope. Try to see what works best for your congregation.

Here is my wish list:

1. **ESL Coordinator(s):** oversees the program; teaches; fills in on any position needed; is the person responsible for answering to the congregation and committees.

2. **Advertising Coordinator:** delivers brochures and advertisements about upcoming events to local places; calls radio, TV, newspaper; sets up information tables in the community and gives explanations of program to passersby; makes announcements in church bulletin and newsletter.

3. **Volunteer Coordinator:** recruits volunteers from church; runs sign-up table at church; calls volunteers to keep them informed; assists in training of volunteers; rewards volunteers with certificates; dinners, etc.; follows up on volunteer concerns; attends volunteer weekly meetings.

4. **Graphic Artist:** designs brochures, advertisements, invitations, certificates.

5. **Social Coordinator:** surveys participants about their interests; sets up quarterly social and service activities; makes all arrangements for activities such as reservations and travel; informs participants and volunteers with information sheets; collects necessary fees; accompanies group and makes sure all goes smoothly.

6. **Administrative Assistant:** collects fees; registers learners; helps order materials; enters learner information on computer; makes certificates; takes attendance; makes copies; runs errands; updates mailing list; makes phone calls; purchases equipment.

7. **Church Secretary:** sends out information to participants on mailing list or waiting list; arranges rooms and equipment at church.

8. **Volunteer Tutors:** work with participants in lab or classes; help participants find appropriate materials; test participants; run conversation or pronunciation groups; develop relationships with participants; go on activities with participants; attend training sessions and biweekly meetings.

9. **Pastor:** runs interference and answers general questions on behalf of ESL program at meetings; sets up class times, dates, rooms, etc.

10. **Christian Educators:** provide daycare and Christian education for participants' children.

11. **Room Setup Person:** moves chairs and tables; sets up video/audio equipment, whiteboards, etc.

12. **Intercessors:** pray for the Holy Spirit's wisdom and leading for developing and running the program; pray for learners' and tutors' needs; pray for the vision and understanding of the church congregation, leaders, etc.

CHAPTER 4

Training for Tutors

Before we begin a discussion about the kind of training a volunteer tutor might receive, it would be helpful for you to know what kind of training professional ESL instructors have. Generally speaking, ESL instructors at adult schools hold a B.A. or B.S degree, while instructors at community colleges hold an M.A.

ESL is a bit of a strange field. Because it has been in the developing stages for a period of time, teachers often come to the field with a variety of different degrees. Recently, the field has become more standardized, and universities are developing specific degrees that address the teaching of English as a Second Language (M.A. in TESOL). Because this is a relatively new phenomenon, many instructors possess degrees in linguistics (the study of other languages and their structures), English literature, Asian or Hispanic studies, reading/literacy, and education. Those are the most typical degrees you will find in the field. There are also shorter certificate programs that an instructor might include as a part of his or her degree program, such as a TESOL certificate program. (The TESOL certificate is a shortened program that includes the essentials of teaching ESL: teaching methodologies, approaches, techniques, and curriculum).

Perhaps you're wondering what kind of training is available for volunteer tutors. If you are attempting to choose a particular training program taught by an ESL professional, it is helpful to know the trainer's educational and experiential background in order to determine what his or her personal biases might be. For example, if a trainer has a linguistics background, he may be more inclined to emphasize language structures in his training program. If a trainer has an education background, she is likely to emphasize good teaching techniques.

I'm speaking in generalizations here, but you need to know who it is that is training you. There is nothing wrong with receiving training from varying organizations. In fact, the more information you have from different sources, the more likely you are to find the resources you will need for your particular situation. Having resources available will keep you from that ugly monster that many tutors have faced—no new ideas!

One of the main reasons I have written this manual is to provide resources so that you don't have to go searching to meet your basic needs. Check out chapter 10 in this book for a list of training books, videos, and audiocassettes. Also, look under the tutor-training programs list in that same chapter. If some training is being offered in your area that you think might help, by all means take advantage of it!

If you can't find an ESL training program in your area, another great resource is net-working with other churches or organizations who have ESL programs at their locations. Ask to speak to their coordinators. Find out what they're doing and what's been successful for them. Ask them where they got their training. Ask them if they would be willing to share any of their printed resources with you. If they have in-house training, ask if you might be able to attend some of their training sessions.

Even if you don't want to run your ESL program exactly like the program you are visiting, you can still get ideas and perhaps find a support network. It's often a great relief to hear another voice on the other end of the line saying, "I know what you mean!" when you describe a difficulty you are having with your program.

You could use the following list of questions as an outline for your own in-house tutor training program if you can't find a suitable training program in your area. These are questions that most tutors will ask; I also indicate where you can find my answers to these questions.

Outline for Tutor Training

1. Is there a need for volunteers to assist in ESL training for internationals in your area? (*See chapter 1.*)

2. Am I qualified to be a volunteer ESL tutor? (*See chapter 1.*)

3. What is ESL anyway? (*See chapter 1*).

4. How do volunteers work in other ESL programs? (*See chapter 9.*)

5. Who are the learners that I will be working with? (*See chapter 3.*)

6. How will I know where to start with the learner? (*See chapter 5.*)

7. What information should I teach the learner? (*See chapter 6.*)

8. What are some activities that I can do with a learner? (*See chapter 4.*)

9. How do I know if I'm really helping the learner or not? (*See chapter 7.*)

10. What if I want to know more? (*See chapter 10.*)

Methods for Teaching English as a Second Language

When interviewing a number of volunteer tutors, I have heard the comment that ESL tutor-training programs often focus too much attention on the theoretical and not enough on the practical side of teaching ESL.

Teaching ESL

I can certainly appreciate this comment if I think of myself doing a task that I am unfamiliar with . . . let's say brain surgery. If, by some strange quirk of fate, I was suddenly whisked into an operating room, done up in a mask and surgical garb, had a scalpel slapped in my hand, and found myself staring at a waiting patient, I wouldn't be asking the surgeon about the various theoretical arguments concerning brain-surgery techniques. All I would say is, "Tell me where to cut!"

Unfortunately, just as brain surgery is not a simple procedure, neither is teaching English as a Second Language. When I look at private ESL programs, I see some quality programs and others that need improvement. I attribute the latter to lack of knowledge by the instructors about the subject area and to ignorance concerning what works and what doesn't work.

Anyone who is teaching ESL (professional or lay person) must have at least a basic understanding of the methods that are currently in use for ESL instruction. Why?

- You will know what you're teaching and why you're teaching it.
- You will have a better idea of what to expect of yourself and your learner.
- You will be able to recognize methods that won't work for you; thus, you and your learner won't be frustrated later because you wasted time and energy.

What are these methods for teaching ESL?

There are about eight major methods or approaches, but I'm going to discuss those that have the most impact on ESL instruction currently. The first, Audio-Lingual, is a method of language teaching that has been used for a number of years; it was probably the method used if you took a foreign-language class in high school or college.

In this method language is viewed as a set of grammatical structures to be modeled by the teacher, copied as precisely as possible by the learner, and drilled until memorized. It is believed that if the learner receives the correct input from the instructor and memorizes the language structures precisely, he will then be able to apply the learned information in new situations. Much repetition and drilling are used as techniques to memorize the material. Substitution drills are also often used. In these drills, the learner is given a base sentence, and she simply changes one vocabulary word in the sentence—for example, "I am a _____." In this example, a learner would be asked to repeat the sentence with different words inserted such as *man, woman, student, doctor.*

Using this method, the teacher directs the learning and acts as a kind of drill sergeant, asking learners to repeat after him. Learners may repeat lists of grammatical structures (such as verb endings) and do written exercises that emphasize these same structures. Dialogues are memorized because it is believed that if a learner has a correct example of a dialogue in her mind, she can apply what she learned from the dialogue to a situation she will encounter in real life.

Although there are some good things about this method, much criticism has been launched against it in recent years. Often the phrases that are taught are useless. For example, the student may learn the phrase, "Here is a car." If a learner walked up to a native English speaker and said, "Here is a car," the native speaker might think, "So what!" The language forms studied in class

should be useful and realistic. A more useful phrase for a learner regarding a car might be, "My car is broken. Can you fix it?"

Another criticism made against this method is that a learner memorizes dialogues in hopes that she will be able to understand and participate in a real dialogue in a public situation. But what happens if the person she is speaking to doesn't use the language structures that the learner memorized in class? The learner is lost and not equipped to handle the situation. A better way to handle this problem is to teach functional language structures that can be applied to any situation. The learner should, for example, know how to ask the speaker to repeat the misunderstood information, to slow down, or to explain a particular vocabulary word.

Another criticism of the Audio-Lingual Method is that it assumes that memorization of a concept means that a learner will apply the information in a new situation. We know from research that this is not necessarily so. A concept called "transfer of learning" applies here: if we want learners to apply some learned information to a new situation, we must help them do it. Learners will not automatically transfer the information themselves, and perhaps they'll never even see the connection between the learned information and the new situation.

Ten years of teaching experience has taught me that these criticisms about this method are true. You can spend an hour drilling a particular skill. But if you ask the learners to apply the information to a new situation, many will stare at you blankly as if you're speaking Greek. What this says is that learners need practice with language structures in a variety of new situations if they are going to be able to apply the information outside of the classroom.

Because I believe these criticisms of the Audio-Lingual Method are well founded, I recommend using what I and many other language professionals consider to be a more effective method of language instruction—the Communicative Method. In it language is viewed as a system to express meaning, and the primary purpose of language is to communicate. Learners use language that is meaningful and aimed at real communication purposes. Activities include getting learners involved in situations where they must share information or negotiate meaning with others.

The teacher acts as a facilitator; he sets up situations and then allows learners to try to communicate within those situations. For example, the instructor may teach the language structure for how to offer suggestions. After modeling and allowing the learners to practice the structure, he will put learners in pairs and have them role-play a situation.

In the role-play one learner may become a supervisor at work, while the other learner becomes the employee. They role-play that they are at a weekly meeting, and the boss asks the employees if they have any suggestions about a particular problem. The learner who is acting as the employee makes a suggestion, and the boss must react to that suggestion in a realistic fashion. Further discussion may ensue, and more suggestions may be made. Using this method, the instructor makes sure that language structures and the situations in which they are practiced are as real as possible.

Does that mean that there is no place for memorization or drills? No; however, these techniques should be used sparingly and for a specific purpose that involves real language.

You'll find many quick-teaching methods that emphasize a lot of grammar (as the Audio-Lingual Method does) to the exclusion of almost everything else. These methods and materials often insist that they are communicative when in fact they are not. Does that mean that learners shouldn't study grammar? No, of course not. But such study should take place in the context of real communication. A learner can study a grammatical concept, but it is our job as instructors to help the learner take that concept and use it in real-life situations. (The materials that I have chosen in chapter 5 reflect this idea to a greater extent.)

I have observed a number of churches using the Total Physical Response (TPR) Method. In it the learner acts out commands given by the instructor. For example, the teacher might say, "Raise your right hand." And the learner raises his right hand.

This method has some advantages, although they are limited. For beginning ESL learners, TPR can be used as listening practice. In addition, the TPR method is an easy way for the teacher to check for comprehension. If the learner doesn't perform the action, the teacher knows immediately that the learner doesn't understand. By giving commands to their classmates, learners can also practice speaking.

The limitations of this method are that all language structures are offered in command form. In the real world we don't walk around commanding everyone to do things for us. You see the problem. This method is also limited because it usually only works well with beginning learners. More advanced learners need to use a variety of language structures.

I prefer to think of TPR as one trick I can pull out of my bag to accomplish a specific task. For example, I might teach beginning learners how to give directions on the street. Then I would set the classroom up like city blocks (using desks) and give learners commands to go down a particular street, to turn left, to stop at the yellow house, and so on, until they reach their destinations. I might also use TPR if I'm teaching grammar, specifically prepositions. After the instructional time I would use TPR as practice, saying such things as, "Put your pencil over your book"; "Put your pencil under your desk"; "Put your pencil in your pocket," etc. There are more training books on TPR listed in the ALTA catalog for those of you who are interested in learning this method in more detail.

In chapter 10 I have listed as many training resources as I could find. Some of these resources may be better than others. I was not able to evaluate each and every one. That's why I've shared the methodological background information with you: so that you can evaluate training materials yourself. I recommend that you first look for training materials that use the Communicative Method. You certainly can use training materials from other organizations who don't use this method, but don't let anyone tell you that his or her methods are the "only correct way" to teach ESL.

As you can probably surmise, there are numerous methods for teaching ESL, each with its advantages and disadvantages. Think about your language-learning experiences in the classroom. Did the way that you learned a foreign language help you to speak it in public with native speakers? Think about the ways that your learners are going to have to use the English in their everyday lives. Choose methods and materials that are going to facilitate that for them.

Lesson Plans for Teaching ESL

In general, most professional ESL instructors use some type of a lesson plan when teaching a class in order to pinpoint the stated learning objectives and to make sure that the information offered in class is presented in an organized fashion. Lesson plans can also assist a teacher in evaluation; examination of the stated objectives and learners' performance should determine if real learning has taken place.

Unfortunately, I have found that many volunteer tutors feel overwhelmed at the thought of creating a lesson plan from scratch. It's true that writing an ESL lesson plan, including learning activities in all four skill areas (reading, writing, listening, and speaking), can be a time-consuming activity.

That's why I recommend that volunteer tutors use ESL textbooks with learners—so that tutors don't have to do everything by themselves. Of course, most textbooks aren't perfect, so you may have to do a little adapting. But if the book has been written by an ESL professional, it should contain the basic elements and will save the tutor a great deal of preparation time.

You will want to check to see if the book has one activity from each of the four skill areas in each lesson. That will be especially necessary if you are teaching beginners, who most likely need to work on all of their English skills. More advanced learners can choose what particular skill(s) they want to work on. If the book doesn't contain an activity from each skill area, perhaps you could add one for whatever skill is missing. Of course, that will take prior planning on your part.

The easiest route to take is to find books that already have a multiple-skills emphasis. But don't get life-skills books (which usually work on all four skills and are for beginners) confused with other texts that are designed to work on only one skill. You don't have to change every book that you work with. In chapter 6 I have tried to recommend books that are good example texts and don't need much changing on your part.

Teaching the Four Basic Skills

Here's my quick list of activities that are often included in teaching the four basic skill areas. You can further develop and add any of these activities to an existing lesson from a textbook that you are currently using.

Reading

1. Prereading skills: make predictions about what will happen in the story.

2. Use comprehension questions for a literal understanding of the story.

3. Discussion questions in small groups to make readers think about the material.

4. Practice skimming, scanning, looking for the main idea.

5. Use vocabulary builders such as flash cards, Concentration.

6. Learn prefixes, suffixes, root words.

7. Give written quizzes using true/false, multiple choice, and fill-in-the-blank exercises.

8. Tell learners half a story; they read the other half and then answer questions.

9. Give learners a list of vocabulary words and have them work in small groups to write a definition for each one.

Writing

1. Look at a painting, discuss a topic, listen to music, watch a movie to give learners something to write about.

2. Ask learners to tell about their families, some interesting experience, etc., in writing.

3. Give learners a story cut up in strips for them to put in order, after which you discuss the different parts of the story, such as the introduction, body, conclusion.

4. Use real-life objects, such as family pictures or cartoon strips, to get learners to write.

5. Write their daily activities in a journal.

Listening

1. Listening dictation: read to learners, and ask them to write down exactly what you say. Then they check their writing for accuracy.

2. Listening cloze: read to learners a piece with some of the words missing. They must fill in the blanks.

3. Oral true/false quizzes: learners hold up a T or F card after you ask the question.

Speaking

1. Have learners discuss topics in pairs, small groups, or large groups.

2. Have learners tell each other personal information, stories, jokes, etc.

3. Have learners go on a "people hunt," in which they have to speak to people in the room to find individuals with specific characteristics (e.g., someone with a blue car).

4. Have learners interview each other and other people outside of the classroom.

Be creative! Think of your own ideas!

Bible-Based ESL Materials

I mentioned earlier that you need to have a lesson plan, but as you'll see in chapter 6, Christian ESL materials and lesson plans are harder to come by. Because of this problem I created a basic lesson plan that offers elements that a conversation class might contain. Then I trained our tutors how to create their own Bible lessons using these elements. I am excited at how well they have done!

Remember, these are people who had no formal training in ESL before they started working with our program (a nurse, a chemist, software engineers, etc.). After they began developing individual lessons and had worked on editing their lessons, we decided that we needed a curriculum so that their lessons would follow each other in a cohesive order. We wanted to communicate the gospel in a clear, step-by-step manner.

We are currently working on a year-long, beginner-seeker curriculum, an intermediate/ advanced-seeker curriculum, an intermediate/advanced-believer curriculum, and an intermediate/advanced-church-membership curriculum. Although these curricula are all still in progress, they are being created by our ESL volunteer tutors (with the exception of the church membership curriculum, which I am developing).

Instead of developing all of your own materials, you may want to use the Bible-based study materials published by Open Door Books (see p. 97). Although these studies were originally developed for a literacy/adult new learner market, they are easy to adapt for ESL and contain many of the ingredients you will need for a successful ESL lesson.

Adapting Open Door Bible Studies
to Intermediate Level ESL Conversation Materials

1. In each chapter, there is an introductory story before the Bible story. Omit the introductory story (or build a separate session around the story, using two sessions for each study) and substitute four or five discussion questions as a prereading activity. The purpose here is to get learners thinking about the story, talking in English, and giving their opinions, right or wrong. For example, in the story "You Must Be a Servant" (Mark 10: 42-45), you could ask questions about work like

   a. What qualities do you think makes a good boss? Make a list with your group. (If you have never had a job, say what qualities you think you would like in a boss.)

   b. What qualities do you think make a bad boss?

   c. Have you ever had a good boss? How did he/she make you feel? Did he/she help you? How?

   d. Have you ever had a bad boss? How did he/she make you feel? Did he/she help you? Why or why not?

2. In the "Words for Study" section, consider adding more vocabulary words to the list. Each story should have at least ten vocabulary words and if the story is longer, about fifteen words. Make a matching exercise with the words and their definitions so learners can interact with the new words. Include Bible jargon, idioms, phrasal verbs (pick up), and any words you know that your learners won't know.

3. The "About God's Word" section should be answered and discussed in small discussion groups with a large group summary.

4. After the preceding section, add a "Listening Dictation" section taken from the Bible passage. Choose the most important part of the story that you want your learners to remember.

5. Again, divide up into small discussion groups for the "Think About It" section, with a large group summary. You might want to add a few questions that relate back to your prereading questions. For example, apply the "being a servant" concept back to the work situation to help your students get the Bible concept back into their real world.

The following is the general lesson plan that I developed and gave to our tutors. You are welcome to use this format as your lesson plan if you would like—either in developing your own materials or adapting others.

Conversation Lesson

1. **Introduction:** The teacher prepares learners by telling them what topic to expect in the lesson (large group).

2. **Conversation Questions:** These are general-interest questions just to get the learners to start thinking. The answers are simply learners' opinions. They aren't right or wrong (discussion in small groups of four or in pairs).

3. **Vocabulary:** These can be matching exercises, fill in the blanks, or a crossword puzzle. (Learners work in pairs and help each other. Check answers as a large group when pairs are finished with the exercise.)

4. **Reading:** Learners read the Bible or lesson materials silently to themselves. (Don't do round-robin reading, in which each learner reads one sentence out loud.)

5. **Conversation Questions:** These questions are actually comprehension questions to see if the learner understood what he read. They are literal and have right and wrong answers. (Discuss in small groups of four or in pairs. Check answers as a large group when pairs are finished.)

6. **Pronunciation:** These are vocabulary words taken from the story. (Learners work in pairs and help each other do the exercise. You can have everyone repeat these words after you, as a large group, after learners have finished the exercise.)

7. **Listening:** The teacher asks the learners true or false questions about the story while the learners hold up a T or F card (index cards) to indicate their answers. (This exercise can be done as a large group.) Another listening activity to use is a listening cloze, in which the teacher reads the story to the learners three times while learners fill in the empty blanks of a copy of the story with some of the missing words (can be done as a large group too). You may need to read the story more slowly for beginners. Finally, learners look at the actual story and correct their spelling mistakes, etc.

8. **Writing:** This activity is optional in your lesson. Often we have not used it in our lessons because learners have requested conversation most of the time. I want to include this activity, though, in case you would like to add a writing element. You may ask learners to write on a topic related to the lesson. Usually you'll need to provide some prompting questions to get your learners started or they will just stare at you blankly. (See the following sample lesson.) You may need to write one of your own examples and show it to them to give them an idea of what you want. Ask beginners to write two or three sentences. Ask intermediate students to write a five-sentence paragraph. Ask advanced learners to write two or three paragraphs, if time permits. You can help them edit their writing individually as they finish.

9. **Conversation:** The purpose of the conversation section is to apply biblical concepts to the learners' own personal lives. This discussion can and should include learners' personal opinions. (Discussion should be in small groups or in pairs, with a large group discussion following.)

10. **Conclusion:** The teacher can make sure that the group learned the biblical concepts at this time by presenting those concepts as a final summary to the story.

The following is a sample lesson, which we have actually used in our intermediate/advanced-seeker-conversation class. The reading comes from the Contemporary English Bible. The video we use is *Jesus Video* from Campus Crusade.

We often watch the video with the sound off, and I talk learners through the story, or I ask them observation questions like the following: What is the man doing? How does the man look? Happy? Sad? Why do you think he looks like that? We watch with the sound off for these reasons: the video is too hard for learners—the vocabulary too large, the speaking rate too fast, and the Bible translation too difficult.

We're thinking about redubbing the video for ESL instruction by reading from the Contemporary English version so that it will match the students' written lessons and be more easily understood. But this is another project that remains undone at the current time!

Sample Lesson

Note: I made a copy of the following worksheets for each learner.

Jesus' Friends Learn to Pray
(Luke 11:1-4)

This story is about a group of Jesus' friends. One friend heard Jesus praying and asked Jesus to teach all of them how to pray.

Conversation Questions

Read the following statements by yourself. Then write a number in each blank that shows your opinion. After you have written numbers in the blanks, discuss your answers with your group and give reasons for why you wrote the numbers you did. Your teacher will give you the correct answers later. When you have finished discussing the questions in Section A with your group, you may go on to section B.

Section A

1. _____ percent of Americans pray once a week.

2. _____ percent of Americans pray once a day.

3. In the Bible there are _____ (number) prayers in which people are asking God to do something for them. God gives _____ (number) answers to these prayers. God's answer rate for these prayers is about _____ percent.

Section B

1. With your group make a list of things that you think people pray for most often.

2. How often do you think God answers people's prayers? (Give a percentage.)

3. Do you think that God will answer you if you pray for *anything?*

4. What answers do you think God normally gives people to their prayers? (Yes, no, maybe)

5. How often do you think a person should pray?

6. To get an answer to your prayer, do you think it matters *who* you pray to?

Vocabulary Words

Match the correct vocabulary word with the correct definition.
Write the proper letters in the blanks.

1. _____ disciple

2. _____ Lord

3. _____ pray

4. _____ follower

5. _____ in this way

6. _____ honor

7. _____ set up

8. _____ kingdom

9. _____ forgive

10. _____ sin

11. _____ keep us

12. _____ tempted

a. respect

b. to strongly want to do something wrong

c. to accept that someone did wrong to you but you choose to love him anyway

d. to talk to God

e. king, ruler, leader

f. one of Jesus' friends

g. area that is controlled by a king

h. like this, using this example

i. someone who does what a leader asks him to do

j. protect us

k. choosing to do something we know is wrong

l. to start, to organize, or to arrange

Reading/Video

Silently read the story on page 1074, chapter 11, verses 1-4.
Watch the video with your class.

Conversation

Discuss these questions with the group to help you understand the story better.

1. Why do you think Jesus' friend asked Jesus to teach him how to pray?

2. Do you think Jesus was happy to teach his friends?

3. In verse 2 Jesus says, "Father, help us to honor your name."
    a. Whose name did Jesus say his friends should honor?
    b. In your opinion how can we show honor to someone? (Give examples.)

4. In verse 2 Jesus says, "Come and set up your kingdom."
    a. Who is Jesus talking about?
    b. God's kingdom is God's government or ruling of the world. Can you guess how God rules the world differently from the way people run the world? (Think about some governments in different countries. Compare them to each other and then compare them to what you think God's way is. What motivates people? What motivates God?)

5. In verse 3 Jesus says, "Give us each day the food we need."
    a. Do you think Jesus was only talking about food? What other things do you think God might give us?
    b. Why do you think Jesus said, "Give us *each day*"? Why didn't Jesus tell his friends to ask God for things once a week, once a month, or once a year?

6. In verse 4 Jesus says, "Forgive us our sins as we forgive everyone who has done wrong to us."
    a. Why do you think that Jesus wanted his friends to ask God for forgiveness?
    b. Is it necessary for us to forgive other people? Why or why not?

7. In verse 6 Jesus says, "Keep us from being tempted."
    a. Why do you think Jesus told his friends to pray about being tempted to do something wrong?
    b. Why do you think Jesus didn't just say, "Be strong! You can do it yourself! Just be a good person!"?

Pronunciation

- With a partner draw lines between the syllables in each word and then write in the blank how many syllables are in the word. If the word has only one syllable, write down (1). If there are two or three words together, write down how many syllables there are in all of the words together.
- Practice saying each word with your partner.
- Your teacher will give you the answers and help you practice saying the words after you and your partner finish the exercise.

1.	disciple	____	7.	set up	____
2.	Lord	____	8.	kingdom	____
3.	pray	____	9.	forgive	____
4.	follower	____	10.	sin	____
5.	in this way	____	11.	keep us	____
6.	honor	____	12.	tempted	____

Listening

Listen to the story as your teacher reads it. Write down the words that you hear, one word in each blank. Your teacher will repeat the story three times. After you listen and write down your answers, check your writing for the correct words by looking in your Bible.

When Jesus had _____ praying, one of his _____ said to him, "Lord,

_____ us to pray, _____ as John taught _____ followers to pray."

So Jesus _____ them, "Pray in this way: _____, help us to _____

your name. Come and _____ _____ your _____. Give us

_____ day the food we need. _____ our sins, as we forgive _____

who has done _____ to us . . . and _____ us _____ being _____."

44

Writing

Working with a partner, write one prayer using Jesus' prayer as an example.
Use these statements to help you write.

1. Start your prayer by writing "Dear God."

2. Write down one sentence that says something about giving honor to God.

3. Write down one sentence that asks God to help you to want to follow him.

4. Write down several things that you want to ask God to give you.

5. Write down one thing that you want God to forgive you for.

6. Write down one thing that you feel tempted about and want God's help for.

7. Write one sentence thanking God for his help.

8. Finish your prayer by writing "In Jesus name, Amen."

Large Group Conversation

Read your prayer(s) for the class. Then discuss these questions.

1. How were each of the prayers that you wrote the same?

2. How were each of the prayers that you wrote different?

3. Look at question number 1 in section B on page 1. Compare your list of what people often pray for with the prayer that you just wrote. Do the list and the prayer have some things in common? How are the list and the prayer different?

4. What does this information tell you about people? What does this information tell you about God?

In this lesson we learned the following:
- God's model for praying.
- That praying is more than just asking God for things.
- That prayer is also thanking God and giving God respect.
- That it is important *who* you pray to if you want an answer.
- That it is important to have established a relationship with God if you want him to answer your prayers.

Language and Intercultural Training Material: Tips for Church Councils

Having a good lesson plan is essential to teach ESL, but it is still not enough if you want to work successfully with your learners. Sometimes learners will do things that you don't anticipate. When you ask them to participate in what you see as normal classroom activities, they won't understand what you want from them. Sometimes learners will do something that surprises or irritates you, or vice versa. Many of the things that happen in the classroom are based upon cultural expectations—theirs or yours.

Challenges in the classroom will not all be cultural in nature; some will be educational. You might have questions about how often you should correct a learner when she makes a mistake. You might have problems pacing your lesson and run out of material to teach before the class period is over. You may ask a question and get no response and wonder what happened.

There are a lot of things to remember when you're teaching ESL learners. There is no way I could possibly list all that you need to know, but I want to at least give you some cultural and educational ideas to get you started. You and your team can figure out more ways to handle classroom issues when they arise.

The following information contains language and intercultural training material that we gave to our church council because they deal with our ESL learners who join the church. The information is useful for many people who normally deal with ESL individuals in the church: tutors, deacons, elders, secretaries, or church members in general. Some of the information is specifically aimed at Asians. You can either use it or look for information specific to the ESL individuals whom you are serving and create your own materials. Most of the information discussed here applies to ESL individuals from different countries.

Language and Intercultural Tips for Church Council

Speaking with Second-Language Learners

1. Try to make a guess the first time you speak to an individual about his English-speaking abilities. That will help you to tailor your speech accordingly.

   If the person is a *beginner*, either she will not understand anything you say or she will understand basic questions about herself and everyday topics, but she will only be able to answer in one-word responses or short phrases.

   If he is an *intermediate*, he will be able to answer everyday questions easily. He will also be able to elaborate somewhat and/or maintain the flow of conversation. He will usually require clarification of some words that are new to him.

   If the learner is *advanced*, she will usually understand all questions and will maintain the conversation. She will rarely have to search for a vocabulary word, and grammatical problems are infrequent. You usually will have very few problems communicating with this learner.

   Most of the learners that you will be dealing with will be intermediate or advanced, since to get in your parish they must have completed the Discovery Class (our church membership class). I include the information about beginners because, when visiting a home, you may meet other family members who are beginners.

2. If it seems like the person is having a hard time understanding you, speak slowly.

46

3. If the person looks puzzled, repeat yourself using easy words.

4. Avoid using slang and idioms when possible.

5. Speak loudly enough so that the person can hear you clearly.

6. Simplify your sentence structure if necessary. Use subject-plus-verb-plus-object forms. Avoid dependent clauses, conditionals, etc., especially with beginners. For example, instead of saying, "Depending on the weather report for next Sunday, we will or will not have the church picnic," just say, "On Sunday, the weather is good, we have the picnic. The weather is bad, we don't have it." You might feel strange talking this way if you're not used to it, but you will be doing your learner a big favor. If getting your idea across is your goal, this is the way to make sure the learner understands what you mean. There will be plenty of time later on in English class for the learner to study and learn to use the proper grammatical structures.

7. Be patient when waiting for the person's answers to your questions. During pauses in the conversation the learner is often translating from his language into English and searching for the correct vocabulary word, grammatical structure, or pronunciation. It takes a little longer than usual to have a conversation with a second-language learner, but it's well worth the wait!

8. Be a good guesser! Second-language learners often leave out prepositions (of, at, in, etc.) and articles (a, an, the). They use essential words like nouns and verbs when speaking. For example, a learner might say, "I see Mary church

yesterday." They also often use the easiest grammatical tenses—present and past. Note the example above. You will need to guess and fill in the blanks in your mind when speaking with these learners.

9. Remember that when the second-language learner is speaking, the ideas being communicated may sound simplistic, but you're still dealing with an adult. Don't talk down to him as you would to a child. Often the learner is trying to express complex concepts with a minimal internal dictionary. Assume that he is an intelligent individual and guess at his meanings when you're not sure what he means.

10. Ask questions. If you're not clear about what was said, be sure to ask the person to repeat herself. Also, ask questions to make sure the person understood you. Sometimes beginning learners will answer yes to everything you say because they are too embarrassed to tell you that they don't understand what you mean. If you're dealing with a beginner, ask specific questions and try to get her to answer with the information so that you can see if the information was absorbed. For example, don't ask, "Will you come to the church on Sunday at 9 a.m.?" (To which the learner would simply answer, "Yes.") Instead ask, "What day will you come to the church?" (To which she might answer, "Sunday.") Then ask, "What time will you come on Sunday?" (To which she might answer, "Nine-o-clock.") You get the idea.

11. If you can't understand the person's pronunciation, guess. Many times the second-language speaker is off by just one letter. He may say, "Can I use your

pan?" when in fact he means, "Can I use your pen?" Many learners from southeast Asia cut off the last letters of a word. For example, "dog" becomes "do," church becomes "chu." Make guesses based on the context of your conversation. If you still can't understand what he is saying, ask him to spell it or write it down. That often helps to remedy this problem.

Telephone Conversations with Second-Language Learners

1. Don't be concerned if the person answers the phone in his native language. Just speak slowly and clearly. The person will switch to English when he hears that you are a native speaker. If someone answers who does not speak English, you might hear a stuttering, "I no speak English," or "He no here." Sometimes a nonspeaker (oftentimes an elderly person) will just hang up on you. If you can, try to find out what time the individual that you want to speak to will be at home and call back then. Also, a non-English speaker may answer in his native tongue. Upon hearing you, he may not answer but will leave the phone immediately. In the background you will hear him shouting in his native language for whoever in the house speaks English. Just be patient and don't hang up even though you don't understand what they are saying. Oftentimes a young person who has learned English in school will get on the line after a few minutes and act as your translator.

2. Again, speak slowly and clearly and follow the tips found in section 1 above. These rules apply *even more* when you are speaking on the phone because the learner cannot see your face to understand your expression and cannot

see your lips to understand your pronunciation.

3. When in doubt, ask questions that check for understanding, and spell critical information that is unclear due to pronunciation difficulties.

Home Visits with Second-Language Learners

1. State the purpose of your visit. Let the learner know that your visit is just a normal procedure of the church to help individuals.

2. Let her know how long you are planning to stay.

3. When you go to the house, if the person gives you a slight bow or head nod, do the same back to him. If the person offers you his hand, then shake hands.

4. Take off your shoes and leave them at the door. (Usually you will see a pile of shoes there already.) If slippers are offered to you, put them on and follow your host to the living room.

5. Your host may or may not offer you something to eat or drink. That will probably depend on how Westernized the individual is. Accept or don't as you please.

6. Usually you will be stared at expectantly and silently to see what you want. Other family members may also look at you curiously. Start right in saying what you want to say and be friendly with other family members.

7. When you leave, your host may bow or nod again. Do the same. Keep some distance between you and don't touch the individual unless she offers her hand

to you. (I'm speaking specifically about Asians here.)

Understanding Second-Language Learners

1. Many ESL learners are nervous to speak with you because they are afraid that you won't understand their English or they won't understand you. Either way, they are afraid of making a fool of themselves. Try to help them relax.

2. You will notice that many of these people are often afraid of being pushed into something. Many have been warned about strange cults and religions before coming to the United States. They don't know if you are going to try to force them into becoming a Christian or into giving money, etc. (Most of the individuals that you meet will have decided to become Christians already, but even these new Christians are still nervous because the whole church system is strange to them.) It is a novel idea for many that you honestly want to help them with no strings attached.

3. We have had a couple of ESL individuals complete the Discovery Class (our church membership class) and yet not become Christians and members of the church. These individuals are still thinking about whether or not to become Christians. If you visit one of them, be especially sensitive to her apprehensive feelings. If she wants to express likes or dislikes about Christianity, just listen and don't argue. Continue to be friendly and show her the love of Christ by your actions.

4. Many times one member of a family will decide to become a Christian and will welcome your visit. Unfortunately, this individual may be living with a spouse or extended family members who are hostile toward Christianity. Some family members view becoming a Christian as a betrayal of the family itself and the individual's native culture. There is not much you can do about this situation except be aware of it, be friendly, and pray for family members.

5. Let individuals know that you can be a contact person for questions and for help with any English problems (for example, phoning a secretary at the church to register for a class, understanding newsletters from the church, etc.).

6. Most of all, you should take the initiative to alleviate ESL learners' fears. Let them know that you're there to help so they needn't feel alone or nervous in their dealings with the church.

Helpful Hints for Teaching ESL

Grouping Your Learners

1. For any conversation activity make sure learners are in small groups or in pairs. Try not to make the group any larger than four learners to ensure that each person in the group gets an opportunity to speak.

2. Activities that don't easily lend themselves to being conversational can be made conversational. For example, try putting learners in pairs when they are working on a vocabulary-matching exercise. Even though they are working on a written paper together, they must speak and help each other get the answers. Learners will then kill two birds with one stone: learning new vocabulary words and conversing about them in English.

3. ESL classrooms often use cooperative learning methods. Learners work in groups rather than alone because the purpose of the learning is to communicate. Interacting by yourself

with pencil and paper doesn't help your oral-speaking skills. If a learner wants to practice his speaking skills, he must practice speaking with others.

4. Assist learners in getting into small groups or pairs. Even if you verbally tell learners to get into small groups or work with a partner, often they will just stare back at you. Because they are so used to sitting in neat rows, not talking during class, and working by themselves, you will have to physically show them how the classroom is to be organized. To do so, start moving chairs into circles. Have the learners get up and move around. Learners have to realize that there is nothing sacred about how their classroom furniture is organized. After a while, learners should become used to this style of group learning, and you won't have to work so hard to get them into groups.

5. Try to use large group structures as little as possible because you will want to give every learner an opportunity to speak during class time. For example, only use a large-group structure for first introducing a topic and giving directions for the activities that learners will be doing in their small groups. At the end of the lesson you can pull everyone back together again for a summary of what went on in their small groups.

Speaking with Your Learners

1. Be careful not to talk too much. Remember that you are a facilitator of the learning. Your job is to introduce topics, to give examples of what you want learners to do, to check to make sure that they understand the task by asking specific questions, and then to launch learners off on their own. You can certainly give anecdotal stories to explain what you mean and to have fun with learners. They will love that

because they like getting to know you as a real person. But keep it in the forefront of your mind that the learners are there to practice speaking and that you need to get out of the way. This is a hard balance that all ESL teachers struggle with. Do your best!

2. Watch your speaking speed. Make sure that you don't speak too quickly (especially if you're nervous for any reason). I often ask learners when I am meeting with a class for the first time if I am speaking too fast or too slow for them. I ask them to stop me if they don't understand what I am saying. You should do the same if you are asking learners to do listening activities. For example, in listening dictation, read at a normal or slightly less than normal pace. For beginners, reading even slower than this is better. Ask learners to tell you if the pace is too fast for them. Slowly work learners up to faster speeds over time.

Relating to Your Learners

1. Be honest with learners, especially when you are sharing your faith. If you are struggling with a particular Christian belief, it's okay to share that. You don't always have to look perfect or be in control or be in the teacher mode. Tell your funny stories and be human. The students will love you for it.

2. Relax and let learners ask their hard questions. You can empathize with them as you discuss issues, but you don't always have to have the answers. Let the ESL classroom be a safe place where they can explore what it means to be a Christian in the real world.

Organizing and Pacing Your Lesson

1. Try to let learners know what is coming in the lesson by giving them a written copy of it, writing an outline of the

activities on the board, or at least verbally introducing each activity and tying it to the previous activity.

2. Make sure to write key concepts and vocabulary on the board. Learners often don't catch what you say when it goes by orally. Make sure to reinforce it visually if you want them to remember what you said.

3. Plan more than enough material for a lesson in case learners finish an activity early. It is always better to have too much to do than not enough.

4. Give adequate time for learners to absorb concepts and respond to your questions. Make sure that you wait for learners' answers. Oftentimes they are translating in their heads to formulate a response for you. Don't jump in and answer the question for them right away. Give them time to think.

5. Make sure that you don't rush through activities. Remember that the lesson plan is there to serve you and your learners, not the other way around. If a particular discussion is going well, let it continue. You can learn to stretch some activities and shorten others, depending on your learners' responses and your allotted class time.

Other General Tips

1. How often should you correct learners' mistakes? Will you hurt their self-esteem or seem rude if you correct them too often? If you would ask most learners whether they want the teacher to correct them, adult learners will say that they do. Still, tutors often feel uncomfortable doing so, especially if the learner is making many mistakes in one sentence. The tutor is afraid of hurting the learner's feelings. A tutor might also feel overwhelmed by the number of mistakes being made, wondering where to start in correcting the learner.

I prefer to think of correction on a continuum, with fluency on one end and accuracy on the other. Each learner fits somewhere on that continuum, and it's your job as a tutor to figure out where he is and then to work with him accordingly. For example, you might have one learner who doesn't feel self-conscious about speaking English. He answers your questions and is eager to carry on a conversation with you. He talks freely but makes a lot of pronunciation and grammatical errors. I would determine that he is very fluent in English but not very accurate. For this learner, I might make more corrections. I would ask him to slow down and think about his errors.

If I had another learner who was very quiet and didn't speak much because she was constantly monitoring her speech to see if she had every grammatical structure correct before she would say anything at all, I would determine that this learner was very accurate but not very fluent and relaxed with English. I might just encourage her to speak and get her ideas across and not worry so much about mistakes. If she becomes more fluent and relaxed, then I would be more vigilant in correcting her mistakes.

You cannot correct every mistake the learner makes even if the learner tells you that he wants you to correct every mistake. This is an impossible expectation that the learner sometimes makes of the tutor. I would encourage you to look instead for patterns of mistakes being made.

Since this is easiest to first do in writing, let me use a writing example to show you what I mean. After a learner has written something—say a letter—look at his mistakes and see if you can find patterns. Does he keep making errors with the same grammatical concept? For example, do five out of ten of his errors have to do with tense? Does he always speak in the present tense and never change to another tense? This pattern tells you that if you teach him about tenses, you may be able to correct about 50 percent of the errors he regularly makes. I don't mean to over-simplify about how difficult it sometimes is to correct learners' mistakes, but this is a place for you to start without getting overwhelmed. Also, if you're teaching a class, apply the same principle. You can't correct every person's mistakes in a class of thirty learners, but you can pick out their top ten errors as a class and work on those.

2. What if learners keep translating what you say into their own language for each other? This is a problem that usually takes place in a beginner class. With beginners I am much more lenient. I let them translate for each other at first. After we have covered a subject several times and I know they have been exposed to how to say a particular phrase in English, then I push them a little more to say the phrase in English.

I don't expect them to say in English what I haven't taught them or what they don't understand. Consequently, if they translate a concept I am teaching for the first time into their own language for others who may not understand, I usually let it go. If, however, a learner always translates for others, and the others are becoming very dependent on that classmate to tell them everything,

I try to stop it. I want each person to learn for himself. A little help now and then is okay, but I don't want some learners to develop a pattern of dependency on others. Usually this problem goes away as learners become more advanced in their usage of English.

3. When using handouts and books—for all learners but especially for beginners—physically point to the part of the book that you want them to look at. Open the book to the correct page and show them the page number. Walk around and check to see if everyone is on the same page. Don't assume anything. If you have several handouts, give them to learners one at a time so they don't get confused or distracted by another page. Again, as learners advance, this situation is less of a problem.

4. After a speaking exercise in which learners have been in groups talking, you will need to get their attention again by raising your voice, holding your forefinger to your lips, or using some other signal that you feel comfortable with to quiet them. Make sure you have everyone's attention before going on to the next part of your lesson.

5. With all ESL learners, but especially with beginners, you can use a lot of panto-mime and visual aids to get your point across. Be an actor and use plenty of pictures.

6. If you just can't seem to get the meaning of a word across to learners, don't give up. This is the time to ask them to look up the word in their own bilingual dictionary.

7. When you're talking about an idea, do as much as you can to relate that idea back to the learner's own culture. For

example, you could say, "In Canada, many people think . . . What do people in your country think about that?" You can help the learner transfer new ideas into a context that he can more easily relate to from his own background. By doing so, you'll learn something new too about the people you are working with.

8. What if learners won't talk in groups? Some learners say that they don't want to work with others. They only want to get the correct answer from the teacher. This problem arises when learners don't understand that the teacher cannot talk to each person in the class on an individual basis. Also, the teacher does not always have the right answer when people are simply expressing their opinions. The teacher should explain that she provides opportunities for each learner to speak with others, so the learner can hear many other people's thoughts on a subject. I also explain that the purpose of group discussion is not always to get the right answer but to practice speaking and listening to others in English.

9. Keep a beginning, intermediate, and advanced dictionary in your head with ready explanations of new vocabulary words for your learners, depending on their levels. For example, if learners come across the word "remember," and they ask you what it means, what could you say? For a beginner you might say, "Don't forget." For an intermediate learner you might say, "Learn something new and keep it in your brain." For an advanced person you might use an idiom like "Know by heart."

As a training exercise I gave our tutors a list of words and asked them to come up with easy as well as more difficult ways to explain the meanings. Then I had them categorize the meanings that they had thought of into beginning, intermediate, and advanced categories.

10. In discussions you should facilitate. Ask questions to draw learners out. If they don't understand your question, rephrase it in easier words. Give them examples of the kind of answers you are looking for. Ask if they have questions about the subject you are discussing. Compliment a learner on his question or answer. That is especially important to do if a person is a seeker and you are discussing Christian information.

This whole chapter has addressed ESL training for tutors. But I want to add a final note on training for tutors in spiritual matters.

For tutors to be well-rounded and effective team players in an ESL ministry, I believe that they must be well-grounded in basic ESL techniques as well as in spiritual issues. I recommend that tutors take a course in how to share their faith and in how to run seeker small groups. The Willow Creek Association (listed in chapter 10) has great resources for both of those.

Finally, as part of that well-grounding process, I also recommend that tutors have some intercultural/interpersonal communication skills under their belts so that they can better relate to their learners. (See the intercultural reading list in chapter 10.)

Whew! There is a lot to be learned when teaching ESL, and for the good teacher/tutor the learning never ends.

CHAPTER 5

Testing Learners

Initial testing is extremely important in determining who your learner is and what he needs. In medical terms, testing is the tool used for making a diagnosis as well as deciding about treatment options. Imagine the disaster if your doctor didn't test you to find out what was wrong but simply gave you a treatment that most likely didn't apply to your illness! The same is true for the classroom.

During my research for this book, one of the problems that tutors expressed to me most often was not having a tool to determine an individual's English-speaking abilities. I have found that most tutors did not know where to look for an appropriate testing device. And in many cases they didn't even realize that testing was needed.

As I spoke further with tutors, it became apparent to me that many learners were entering an ESL program without being tested to determine their English-speaking level; they were simply being placed in an existing class. As a result, people of varying abilities ended up in the same classroom—a very frustrating situation for both tutor and learner.

In saying all of this, it's not my intention to condemn anyone! If you don't normally work with ESL students, of course you can't be expected to know where to find testing materials. I am saying that it's important for you to test learners when they come to you initially so you know who you are working with.

So then, what test should you use? Is one better than another? These are questions educators ask all the time. Some standardized ESL tests are quite elaborate, requiring a great deal of training to administer. Some are set up to measure very specific things that you and your learner may or may not have studied. Others are quite expensive to purchase. I'm not saying that you shouldn't use these tests. If you want to get the training or study a specific curriculum or don't mind paying a lot, by all means go ahead.

My thinking is this: first, churches usually use volunteer tutors who aren't willing to go through a lengthy training process. And some tutors are afraid that they won't understand the training because previous educational training is assumed. Second, many learners come into an ESL program with their own needs and desires; they might want to study a subject that isn't on the curriculum list and that a specific test doesn't measure. Third, many churches (especially fledgling ministries) operate on a shoestring budget. Taking a large chunk out of the annual budget for testing may not be appropriate.

What most tutors really need, I believe, is a "quick and dirty" assessment of their learner. They need something that will help them discover the learner's needs in a short time, say about ten minutes or less. (Many of the formal tests take close to an hour or more.)

For these reasons I propose a short test of written skills (five minutes) and a short oral interview (five minutes). I have borrowed a testing format as well as testing guidelines from the ABC Adult School in Cerritos, California; however, the tests I have created are my own.

Remember that it is very important to give both written and oral tests since a learner's abilities may be different in these areas. For example, an Asian learner might be very good at grammar and writing but not as good at speaking because she never studied spoken English before she came to this country. In this case you would ask her to consider choosing materials designed to improve conversational skills so that she could excel in all areas of the English language.

You can usually take a registration day or the first day of class to test the individual. If your program is big, consider setting aside one day just for testing. In our language lab we have a testing area, which is the first area learners visit upon registration. The written test can be given to large groups at one time. Make sure you explain the test clearly and have a timer and pencils ready. With large groups you may have to watch out for individuals helping each other. Make sure that you collect all of the tests so that one doesn't escape and get copied. If that happens, you'll have to get a new test!

The oral interview is a little more difficult if you have a large group because you must test learners one at a time. Still, learners tend to accept waiting as part of the process. If you have more than one person interviewing at a time, the process obviously will go more quickly. I use a numbering system in which each learner takes a number and waits his turn in line (in another room preferably so that he can't hear the questions and responses). Use the oral interview guidelines to determine a learner's level. These guidelines may seem a little subjective but they work, especially if the interviews are conducted by the same individual(s). Be sure to familiarize yourself with the guidelines before you give the interview.

Test Scoring Guidelines

Written English Test

Read the story and check each blank for a word that makes sense with the rest of the sentence and the story. If the word is in the wrong grammatical tense, mark it wrong (Mary <u>eat</u> lunch yesterday). If the spelling is wrong, mark it wrong. If a learner makes up a word that is close but isn't in the correct form, mark it wrong (Mary <u>eated</u> lunch yesterday). In other words, if the word is not appropriate or is not grammatically correct, mark it wrong. Sometimes learners' answers will be almost good enough. You will feel that you would like to give them credit, but stick to these guidelines so that everyone is tested equally and fairly.

After you have determined the number of correct answers, use this scoring guide to assign the learner a level.

Total number of correct answers:

0-3   Level 1 (low beginner)

4-9   Level 2 (high beginner)

10-15 Level 3 (low intermediate)

16-19 Level 4 (high intermediate)

20-23 Level 5 (low advanced)

24-26 Level 6 (high advanced)

Let me say a few words about the level system. Levels 1 and 2 are beginning levels. Levels 3 and 4 are intermediate levels. Levels 5 and 6 are advanced levels. Some institutions also use the words "high" and "low" to show further distinction between learners of each level. For example, a level 1 learner would be a low beginner while a level 2 learner would be a high beginner. The same system is true for intermediate and advanced learners. Each institution that you might deal with could have a different numbering system, but I have presented the general system that many schools and book publishers follow.

Oral Interview

Level 1: The learner does not understand anything you ask him.

Level 2: The learner understands basic questions about himself, but he can only answer you back with one- or two-word responses.

Level 3: The learner understands basic questions about himself. He can answer using short phrases. He cannot carry the conversation by himself because of his limited vocabulary. The learner pauses often as he tries to think of the right word, grammatical structure, etc.

Level 4: The learner understands basic questions and can use them with little difficulty. He is able to add extra information to a limited degree. The learner's vocabulary still limits him. Grammatical errors often make it hard for you to understand exactly what he is talking about.

Level 5: The learner is able to communicate freely on basic topics about himself and elaborate without difficulty. He is able to maintain the flow of conversation without many starts and stops. He may ask you to explain more complicated questions. Every now and then he searches for a vocabulary word. Once in a while grammar is a difficulty for him.

Level 6: The learner is native-like in his speaking abilities. He maintains the flow of conversation. He understands what you ask and elaborates readily. Grammar and vocabulary are rarely a problem for him. Every once in a while there are a few errors in his speech, but these errors never impair communication.

Oral Interview Questions

Directions: Do not show this paper to the individual you are testing. Have the person sit across from you while you ask these questions. Ask the exact same questions of each person you test so that the same test will be administered to everyone. As you listen to the person's answers, you can look at the oral interview guidelines to determine the individual's level. Write the level on the "Oral Level" line at the bottom of the written test. Tell the learner to relax—there are no right or wrong answers. Reassure him that you are just listening to his speaking to see what his English level is.

1. What is your name?

2. What country are you from?

3. How long have you been here in the U.S. or Canada?

4. Have you studied English before? Where? How long?

5. What do you do every day?

6. Why did you come to the U.S. or Canada?

7. Why do you want to study English at this church?

Written English Test

Directions: Please read the story below. Some of the words in the story are not there. After you read the story, write one word that you think sounds good in each blank. For example, "Mary is a _____ ." In the blank you could write "woman," "girl," "mother," etc. Any of these words are okay. You will have 5 minutes to finish the test. Please stop when your teacher tells you to stop.

Cathy lives in a _____ house. The house is _____ Baker Street. She lives in the _____ with her mother and _____ brother, John.

The house _____ four bedrooms and a _____ kitchen.

The house has _____ windows in the kitchen. _____ likes to sit in the kitchen and _____ after school. She likes to eat _____ while she studies.

Cathy _____ to cook. There are _____ vegetables and some meat _____ the refrigerator. Cathy cooks _____ with some rice. Her _____ and her brother are very _____ after work.

After dinner _____ and her brother like _____ watch T.V. They watch a _____ show. Cathy's mother _____ a book.

They are _____ happy family. At night, _____ says good-night to _____ family. She goes upstairs _____ into her bedroom. She _____ off the light. Cathy _____ a good life.

Number possible correct: 26

Number correct: _____

Written level: _____

Oral level: _____

CHAPTER 6

Choosing Curriculum and Materials

Choosing the materials you will use in your program can be difficult. Before you choose your materials, you really need to know what your curriculum is going to be. What is your end goal? What do you want your learners to know when they leave your program?

Curriculum can be a particularly sticky issue for churches. Many churches want to add a Christian element into their ESL program, but they are not sure if this is appropriate or not. Let me share how I have tried to approach this issue.

While visiting ESL programs at various churches, I have observed that both Christian and secular materials are being used. And I have listened to debates among people from different denominations about whether using Christian or secular materials is "right" or "wrong." These debates are not limited to nonprofessional tutors. Some of the hottest debates have been among ESL professionals in the church.

So which is right? What kind of materials should each church use? If we use only Christian materials, are we shoving the gospel down learners' throats whether they want it or not? Do we have a captive audience, people who need English so desperately that they'll stay and work with Bible materials just to get any instruction at all? Are we glad about that? Is it fair to promise English instruction—which learners may perceive as secular instruction that will help them in their daily lives—and instead give them Bible studies and stories about Jesus that they don't know what to do with?

On the other hand, do we choose only secular ESL materials because we want to be so careful not to pressure our learners into considering Christianity as a viable way of life for themselves? Then what happens to the command Jesus gave us to teach a dying world the truth about his love and salvation? If we don't provide opportunities for learning about Jesus, then what makes the church different from the secular adult schools or the community colleges? Is it fair to withhold spiritual information from learners that could help them in their everyday lives?

If you're feeling a little hot under the collar right now, that's okay. I'm not going to tell you what kind of ESL materials your church should or shouldn't use. That will be your decision. What I hope to do is present a balanced approach to this issue.

In our ESL programs, we are working with whole people—people who have physical, emotional, and spiritual needs. In our society, we tend to compartmentalize people and send them to different institutions to meet each of these needs. If they are sick, we send them to a doctor. If they have family problems, we send them to a counselor. If they have spiritual needs, we send them to the church. Or do we?

North American Christians are often afraid to offer spiritual information to people who come from other countries because we don't want to push religion on them. We don't want to undermine their culture. We don't want to repeat the mistakes of Christian missionaries in the past. Yet I have discovered that many of the people I come in contact with are interested in Christianity. I have found myself trying to talk someone out of becoming a Christian because I couldn't believe she really understood the implications of this decision. Often I have observed that an ESL learner's biggest problem is that she simply has never had the opportunity to hear about Christianity in a way that she could understand (in simplified English or in her own language) or relate to culturally.

If someone comes to me expressing a desire for spiritual information, I need to ask myself: Do I really believe Christianity can help this person? Is Christianity only for my culture but not for others? Jesus said: "Go and make disciples of all nations . . . teaching them to obey everything I have commanded you" (Matt. 28:19-20). If I want to follow Jesus' commandment, I have an obligation not to withhold valuable spiritual information from people who ask me for help. The real problem for me is how to present that information without attaching my cultural baggage to it. It's like walking a tightrope. But I do believe it is possible to offer the good news of Jesus and be culturally sensitive to my learner at the same time. (Chapter 10 lists further readings that discuss this subject at length.)

Well then, if I am going to meet a learner's spiritual needs, what about her other needs? Are they less important? By no means! Do churches have ministries that help people on a physical or emotional or some other practical level? Of course they do! Soup kitchens and homeless shelters. Money management and parenting classes. Family counseling and after-school childcare. Support groups for single parents and widowers. These are only a few of the many practical services available at the local church level. ESL classes belong on this list as well. Few would argue this point, so let's get back to the original question: What curriculum should we teach, and which materials should we choose?

As a member or attender of my church, I can attend a Bible study or receive pastoral counseling to help me grow spiritually. I can take a money management course or an aerobics class to manage my everyday life. I need both kinds of services because I have different needs. To say that I should only get spiritual training ignores my real everyday fights with money and fat. To say that I should only get help with my everyday needs ignores the fact that God cares about me and wants to help me. I'm a whole person.

As a member of a church, I can *choose* which services I want to use. This ability to choose is the key element for learners in an ESL program. The type of materials used should be based upon the learner's choice. Then, if a learner chooses Christian materials, it is his business. No one has pushed him into it. If he chooses to study secular materials, it is also his business. If we really care about the learner as an individual, we will give him exactly what he asks for and not try to manipulate him.

I propose that we allow learners to choose what they want to study. This allows us to meet the need expressed by the learner and provides the basis for a trusting relationship to develop. We become more credible when we deliver what we promise. I have observed that many times a learner will start out requesting one type of material and then voluntarily switch to the other as he feels the need. Learners enjoy this freedom and tend to feel more comfortable asking for what they want. It's all quite simple. We give learners what we all want—the freedom to choose.

I'm proposing that churches use Christian *and* secular materials. Let learners choose which they want to use. We needn't see ESL instruction as a means to an end—teaching people English long enough to get them saved. And we needn't see teaching English as merely doing good works in our Lord's name. We are called to *teach God's truth* from the Bible and to *love people as they are,* whether they become Christians or not. We are called to *do good to others* because Jesus told us to love our neighbors. We need to do these things without trying to control anyone's life. The result of our efforts will be decided by God and the person we are seeking to help.

This proposal requires a lot more work on your part. You'll need to learn how to use both Christian and secular ESL materials. You'll need to offer a choice to your learner and not try to control what he chooses. You might have to offer two class times for two separate classes. You'll need to regard both teaching the Bible and teaching everyday English as good and desirable.

That isn't easy to do, especially if you have strong views about a certain type of curriculum being better for ESL learners. But no matter which camp you fall into, I ask you to consider the needs of your learners. Jesus understood people as whole beings. He dealt with them by meeting their needs (to be healed physically and to receive forgiveness). I suggest that we follow his example the best way we know how.

Let me share a few examples. In the ESL program at my church, we have one learner who requested Christian ESL materials because she had just become a Christian. She couldn't understand her English Bible but felt she could improve her English and study the Bible at the same time. We are attempting to help her both in her English skills and in her understanding of the Bible. She has gone through membership classes at our church and was recently baptized. If she requests more Bible classes or some secular English course work, we will work with her to obtain her goals.

Another learner came in requesting help with her English. She had studied it in secular programs at the local adult school and at her place of employment. When we asked her if she wanted to use Christian or secular materials, she told us that she was interested in learning more about the Bible because she didn't know much about it.

Today, a year and a half later, her oral English has improved from level 2 to 4, and she has decided to become a Christian. She has also gone through membership classes and was recently baptized. In studying the Bible with her, we discovered that she could use some work on her reading skills. She has also requested help with her grammar. Now she is working with a tutor on these skills using secular materials.

A third learner came into my class one day and said emphatically (before I even got a chance to ask her) that she wanted to learn English but did not want to study the Bible. I gathered that she had had a bad experience with someone knocking on her door and trying to push her to join some religion. She was leery of us, but she really wanted to study English at the church because our time was convenient for her. She said she wanted to improve her English for her job, so I set her up with a small tutoring group working on business English. She has also attended our ESL social activities with the other study groups and has appeared to enjoy the gatherings.

One week, when her tutor was gone, I invited her to study with our intermediate group that was studying the Bible. I warned her that we were studying Christian materials and that she did not have to feel pressured to come. She decided to try it for one week. After the class, she told me that it was interesting and that after she finished studying business English, she might like to try this class. Four months later, she was still studying business English. Two weeks ago, at her own initiative, she started studying the Bible with the intermediate class on Sunday mornings.

My point is this: when learners come to the door, they often know what they want initially. They'll tell us if we'll listen. We need to treat them like the adults they are. Our job is to make a variety of options available and to let them make up their own minds. If they change their minds about what they want midway through the process, we should try to meet those needs as best we can.

Learners may be leery about studying Bible materials in part because they don't equate such study with learning "real" English. That actually could be the case in programs that use traditional Bible study materials and difficult English translations of the Bible. It's important to select materials that are relevant to the learner's everyday life. Most important, materials should incorporate ESL teaching techniques so that in fact the learner will learn English in the process of learning the Bible.

It is my hope that more Christian materials will be written specifically for ESL learners. Instead of teachers using traditional Bible studies as the curriculum, they'll use materials that teach English from the Bible. These materials will truly emphasize all four skill areas of language learning: reading, writing, listening, and speaking. Very few of these materials are available. You'll find that most Christian materials are designed for literacy and/or new readers. So I encourage those of you who are teaching Bible curriculum to develop ESL materials for your learners' sakes. Perhaps in the future we will all benefit from your endeavors.

Okay, you may be saying. This sounds good, but how can I realistically incorporate both Christian and secular materials into an ESL program? A good question, and one I

struggled with too. Here's how we handled it at our church. Remember, it's not the way you have to do it at your location!

I imagined that our ESL program was like a condominium development—going up in stages. The first stage was, of course, meeting the everyday English needs of the learner by teaching secular English materials. The second stage was meeting some of the emotional needs of the learner, such as the need for friendship, by offering social activities that included ESL learners and native English speakers from the church. The third stage was meeting the spiritual needs of the ESL learner by teaching Christian ESL materials.

It was important to me to have ESL learners at church on Sunday mornings so that they could meet and interact with church members. We incorporated ESL classes using Christian materials into the regular church school hours so that ESL learners could feel like anybody else who was attending a church school class.

We started with a Sunday class first simply because I was working at a community college during the week and Sundays were my only free time to teach a class. After the Sunday classes were up and rolling, we started to offer some social activities because we wanted to spend more time together just having fun (the second stage). The social activities have been great opportunities for learners to relax and meet people. We have had game days and numerous parties, gone golfing and bowling, and eaten at restaurants. We plan to go horseback riding and camping soon. We also hope to have a cooking night in which learners and members of the congregation share recipes and cook together.

We started the final stage, teaching secular materials, when I became available on days other than Sundays. We opened a lab on Saturday mornings that learners could use to study whatever materials they chose at their individual English levels. (See chapter 9 for more information on this subject.)

You can see that we started with stage 3, proceeded to stage 2, and finally finished with stage 1. Many of our decisions came out of my time constraints. Remember that there's no right way. You'll have to decide what will work best for your church and which stage you'll want to start with.

What is important is the end result—having a complete program that meets all of the stated needs of your ESL learners. Having a curriculum that includes both Christian and secular materials will help you accomplish this goal.

Recommended Book List

Because tutors have asked me which materials are good and which they should order first for their learners, I have compiled this basic list. It is by no means comprehensive, as you will discover upon reading various ESL publishers' catalogs. The list is simply meant to get you started in the right direction. I've included old standbys that are currently used at many adult schools and community colleges. I've also tried to include materials that I have heard learners request and/or enjoy the most. The level number listed behind the book in parentheses will help you to decide which learners should use this book.

Of course, there are always new materials coming out regularly, so you'll need to be on the mailing lists of various publishers. As you purchase new materials that are not on this list, look for those that use the communicative method and real, everyday language. (See chapter 4 for more information on this subject.) You'll find it extremely helpful to go to the bookstore and look at the books

firsthand before you order them. (For example, the Alta Book Center has a reading room for this purpose. See chapter 10.) Otherwise, ask the publisher or bookstore for an examination copy. Then you can look at the book for several days and return it at no cost if you don't like it. Alta is also good about ordering books for you that aren't listed in its catalog. Make sure you ask them to help you if you find a book that you like!

If a book is part of a series, be sure to choose the correct book for your learner. For example, if books 1, 2, and 3 are for beginning through low-intermediate learners, you would choose book 1 for a level 1 person (LB), book 2 for a level 2 person (HB), and book 3 for a level 3 person (LI).

Recommended Secular ESL Materials

See Alta catalog (order information, p. 96) for all pertinent details. All asterisked items (*) list the publisher in case Alta can't get it for you. See chapter 10 for a list of publishers.

1. **Reading**
   — *Personal Stories* (1, 2)
   — *English with a Smile* (2, 3)
   — *American Holidays* (3, 4)
   — *News for You* (3, 4), New Reader's Press
   — *Reader's Choice* (5, 6)
   — *True Stories in the News* (1-6)

2. **Composition/Writing**
   — *Picture Stories for Beginning Communication* (1, 2)
   — *Please Write* (1, 2)
   — *Practical English Writing Skills* (2, 3, 4)
   — *Writing Academic English* (4, 5)
   — *Insights into Academic Writing* (5, 6)

3. Grammar

— *Side by Side* (1)
— *Basic English Grammar* (2, 3, 4)
— *Fundamentals of English Grammar* (3, 4, 5)
— *Understanding and Using English Grammar* (4, 5, 6)

4. Listening

— *HearSay* (1, 2)
— *Active Listening* (3)
— *Whadayasay* (3)
— *Listening Tasks* (3, 4)
— *Face the Issues* (4)
— *Consider the Issues* (4, 5, 6)
— *Raise the Issues* (5, 6)

5. Conversation

— *New Person to Person* (1-4)
— *American Scenes* (3, 4)
— *Talk About Values* (3, 4)
— *Great Ideas: Listening and Speaking Activities for Students of American English* (3, 4)
— *Stories from Lake Wobegon* (4, 5, 6)
— *Getting Started in Public Speaking* (5, 6)

6. Pronunciation

— *Sounds Easy* (1, 2)
— *Clear Speech* (3, 4)
— *Phrase by Phrase* (3, 4)
— *Pronunciation Exercises for Advanced Learners of ESL* (5, 6)

7. Idioms

— *Getting Along with Idioms* (2, 3)
— *101 American English Idioms* (2, 3)
— *All Clear* (3, 4)
— *Street Talk* (3-6)
— *Moving Ahead with Idioms* (4, 5)

8. Life Skills/Survival English

— *Interchange* (1, 2, 3)
— *Life Prints* (1, 2, 3), New Reader's Press
— *People Talking* (3, 4, 5)

9. Work-Related English

— *Basic Telephone Training* (2, 3)
— *Business Interactions* (3, 4, 5)
— *Living and Working in America* (3, 4)
— *Business Correspondence* (4)

10. Reference

— *Oxford Picture Dictionary*
— Any thesaurus
— Any dictionary

11. TOEFL

— These are college entrance test preparation materials for advanced learners only. This test is the ESL learner's equivalent of our ACT or SAT tests taken by high school students.
— *Longman Preparation Course for TOEFL* (4, 5, 6)

12. Literacy

Order these materials only if you have a second-language learner who cannot read and write in his own language as well as in English. These books have lots of pictures.

13. Software

If you have a number of computers, you might need to pay for a site license to put the software on all of your computers legally. Ask the publisher or distributor when you order.

— *Crossword Challenge* (1-4)
— *Word Attack* (3-6), can be found at your local computer store
— *Grammar Mastery* (1-6)
— *MacEnglish for Pronunciation* (check with a Macintosh dealer)
— *Crossword Master* (you can make crossword puzzles for the learner)

14. **Teacher Resource**
    — *Designing Tasks for the Communicative Classroom,* Nunan, David (listed in chapter 10). This book has a good list of activities for the four basic skill areas for all English levels in Appendix C; it also has a good overview of ESL methods in Appendix B.

Recommended Christian ESL Materials

1. **Reading**
   — Good News for New Readers series (1, 2, 3), American Bible Society

   — Life Stories series (3, 4), CRC Publications

   — Bible Studies series (3, 4), CRC Publications

   — Faith Questions series (3, 4), CRC Publications

   — *Friendship with God,* Willow Creek Association

2. **Bibles**
Contemporary English Version (3-6), American Bible Society

(This is one of the best easy-to-read Bibles in terms of simple sentence structure, vocabulary words, and conversational English. This Bible doesn't speak down to adult learners, as some children's versions might.)

New International Reader's Version (2, 3), Zondervan; International Bible Society

The easy readability of this version makes it ideal for adults who are learning English as a second language. The NIrV is written at a third-grade reading level and based on the best-selling New International Version.

3. **Reference**
   — *God's Awesome Promises* (3-6), Word Publishing; use in conjunction with an easy Bible
   — *Bible Dictionary,* All Nations Literature
   — *Peace with God* booklets (3-6); use the picture side to explain
   — Any Bible concordance

4. **Videos**
   — *The Jesus Video* (1-6, if you use it with the sound off and talk beginners through it), Multi-Language Media
   — The Living Bible series (Christian Book Stores)
   — *The Book of Matthew* and *The Book of Acts*

5. **Discipleship Materials**
   — Growing in Christ series, NavPress
   — *Thirty Discipleship Exercises* (book and video), Billy Graham Association
   — Serendipity series, Christian bookstores
   — *Discussion Manual for Student Discipleship,* Shepherd Ministries
   — Check the latest CETC newsletter for more book listings
   — Look for TPR Bible lessons for beginners put out by NavPress

Note: Because we want ESL learners who are new Christians to be discipled as quickly as possible, and we want them to be able to learn from the Bible themselves, we have also ordered Christian materials in their first languages.

Learners can check out a variety of books, videos, and music on audiocassettes for a week from our ESL library. We also have evangelistic materials in various languages so that learners can hear the gospel in a language they understand. (In addition, each learner receives a gospel tract in English and in his native language upon entering the ESL program.) Learners have eaten the lending library up like sliced bread, especially the videos! Many of these materials are available from Multi-Language Media.

CHAPTER 7

Evaluating Your Program

Some educational programs have elaborate exit testing procedures to validate that, in fact, learning has taken place. While there is certainly nothing wrong with this, a simpler way to evaluate might be more appropriate for church ESL programs. First, we do not have to answer to the government in evaluating our programs. Also, some of the testing procedures used in standard educational programs require a great deal of training for teachers to administer properly.

I believe we need to answer first and foremost to our learners and to the tutors who are directly involved in the instructional process. Therefore, though the process is subjective, I suggest using questionnaires like the following, which can be given to learners and tutors at the end of a class or midway through the session to determine successful or unsuccessful practices. The first questionnaire is intended to be used for a language-laboratory setting; the other for a more traditional classroom setting using Christian materials.

As you will see, some of the questions are highly specific to my church's activities. Feel free to adapt the questionnaire to reflect the activities in your church. Also, if you don't feel comfortable asking some of the questions, simply delete them or add your own.

With some groups, especially beginners or those learners who don't feel comfortable with a lot of writing, you may want to survey them orally as a group and write down their responses.

After you receive written or verbal responses, make sure you keep what learners and tutors say is good in your program, and look for new ideas and activities to try in those areas that need improvement. The evaluation process has usually been an encouraging experience for me as I find out that we really are helping learners and meeting their needs. I hope that you find this too!

Participant Evaluation Form (Language Laboratory Setting)

1. What skills did you want to work on when you signed up for the lab? (Please circle one or two.)

   a. reading
   b. writing
   c. listening
   d. conversation
   e. pronunciation
   f. life skills

2. Do you think that coming to the lab helped you advance in this skill? Why or why not?

   _____

   _____

3. Do you think that ___ hours a week is enough lab time for you to study English? Do you think the lab should be open more time, less time, or about the same amount of time per week?

   _____

   _____

4. Were the lab hours convenient for you? If not, what time would have been more convenient?

   _____

   _____

5. What did you like best about the lab?

   _____

   _____

6. What would you like to change about the lab?

   _____

   _____

7. Do you think the price for the lab is okay? Why or why not?

   _____

   _____

8. Were the assistants friendly and helpful?

   _____

   _____

9. Were the assistants prepared to help you? Could they answer your questions?

   _____

   _____

10. If you had a specific problem with English, did you feel comfortable asking the assistants for help? Why or why not?

    _____

    _____

11. Did you learn anything at the lab? What was it?

    _____

    _____

12. Did you learn more, less, or about the same amount of English at the lab as you have learned in other English programs? Why do you think this is true?

_____

_____

13. Did you use the childcare at church?

_____

_____

14. Were there any problems with the child-care?

_____

_____

15. Would you recommend the lab to a friend or family member? Why or why not?

_____

_____

16. Have you made any new friends at the lab?

_____

_____

17. Did you have a hard time finding the church or the lab at the church?

_____

_____

18. How did you hear about the lab? (Please circle one.)

   a. advertisement/brochure

   b. radio

   c. television

   d. newspaper

   e. friend or family member

   f. other (Please explain.)

_____

_____

Thank you for your help!

Participant Evaluation Form (Traditional Classroom Setting)

1. What skills did you want to work on when you signed up for this class? (Please circle one or two.)

   a. reading
   b. writing
   c. listening
   d. conversation
   e. pronunciation

2. Do you think that this class has helped you advance in this skill? Why or why not?

   _____

3. Do you think that you got enough practice time for this skill during class?

   _____

4. Do you think that ___ hours is enough class time? Would you want more time per week or less?

   _____

5. What did you like best about this class?

   _____

6. What would you like to change about this class?

   _____

7. Do you think the price for this class is okay? Why or why not?

   _____

8. Was the teacher prepared?

   _____

9. Did you learn anything in this class? If so, what was it?

   _____

10. Were the teacher and the assistants friendly?

    _____

11. Did you mind studying English from the Bible?

    _____

12. Did you use the childcare at church?

    _____

13. Were there any problems with the childcare?

    _____

14. Which learning activities did you like the most? (Please check.)
    ___ music
    ___ drama
    ___ listening dictation
    ___ church concerts
    ___ games
    ___ learning new vocabulary
    ___ conversation
    ___ pronunciation
    ___ meeting Americans
    ___ tour of the church
    ___ watching the Jesus video

15. If you had a personal problem, would you feel comfortable talking with the teacher or assistants and asking them for help or asking them to pray for you? Why or why not?

    _____

16. Did the teacher and the assistants help you learn the materials? How?

_____

17. Would you recommend this class to a friend or family member? Why or why not?

_____

18. Which activities did you enjoy the most? (Please circle one or more.)
    a. camping
    b. bowling
    c. game night
    d. horseback riding
    e. Christmas party
    f. cooking
    g. roller skating
    h. hiking
    i. ice skating

19. Is there another activity you would like to try next time?

_____

20. Is there anything that you would like to attend at the church or have more information about? (Please circle one or more.)
    a. baptism
    b. communion service
    c. singing in the church (concerts, etc.)
    d. women's retreat
    e. men's retreat
    f. couple's retreat
    g. Discovery class
    h. Fall Family Festival
    i. holiday programs (Christmas, Easter, Thanksgiving, etc.)
    j. dramas

    k. Sunday morning worship service
    l. baby dedication
    m. library
    n. a small group
    o. family camp
    p. sports

21. Have you made any new friends in this group? Why or why not?

_____

22. Is there anything that you want to learn about Christianity or about Christian people?

_____

23. Do you want to meet more American people in the church? If so, why?

_____

24. Did you have a hard time finding the church or the classroom at the church?

_____

25. How did you hear about this class?

_____

26. Is this class better, worse, or about the same as other English classes you have taken in the past at other schools? How?

_____

27. Would you feel comfortable going to a Sunday morning church service by yourself? Why or why not?

_____

Thank you for your help!

Tutor Evaluation Form

1. What have you liked the most about teaching ESL, either in the lab or in the classroom?

   _____

   _____

2. What areas have been difficult for you?

   _____

   _____

3. Are there any areas that you would like more training in? If so, what are they?

   _____

   _____

4. Have you noticed any ways that you think we might improve the program? If so, what are they?

   _____

   _____

5. Has the time commitment been okay for you, or has it been too much, too little, etc.?

   _____

   _____

6. Have you felt supported in terms of encouragement, resources, training, sharing with other tutors and coordinator, prayer support, etc.? Why or why not?

   _____

   _____

7. Would you recommend ESL tutoring in this church to another person from our congregation? Why or why not?

   _____

   _____

CHAPTER 8

Customizing to Meet Learners' Needs

If you haven't picked up on it yet, I'm an advocate of each church finding out what works for them and then doing it. I truly believe that carbon copies of ESL programs do not transfer well to different locations because there are too many variables involved in developing a program that works.

I am also a great believer in service. Sometimes it's hard to get someone to pay attention to your specific needs when you have a problem. I discovered this on a recent trip to the doctor! When you have a problem, you want someone who will listen to you and give you what you need instead of putting you through a standard procedure that may or may not work in your situation.

ESL learners want this too. When they get someone to actually hear what they are saying and have that person work on their problem, it's like a breath of fresh air. They want to be included in their own learning process. They know what they struggle with. They know what they need.

Often, because of the sheer numbers of ESL learners in an adult school or community college program, it is easy for a learner to get lost in the crowd and not get her individual needs met. When I taught in the public school system, I had learners slip between the cracks because I just wasn't able to meet so many needs by myself. There were also times when I found myself teaching a curriculum or using materials that both the learners and I knew weren't working or weren't fulfilling their needs, but we had to continue using them because

someone higher up than both of us had decided that they were appropriate. Learners would complain, and I was stuck between them and the administration.

I want you to know that church ESL programs can make a real difference—just by listening to the learner. Learners often get lost in the shuffle while others are deciding what's best for them. Our job as English tutors in the church is not to control learners but to serve them. We need to put the learning back in their hands. Just because I am a professional ESL instructor doesn't mean that I always know what is best for a learner. I may have some good guesses, but each person's difficulties and desires are specific. It is our job to work with learners in order to meet those needs.

How do we do that? To start with, each program is made up of individuals from different countries, depending on who lives around the church. As I think of different churches here in the Bay area, I can imagine ESL programs that look quite different. For example, one church has many Japanese professionals living in the area. They are often interested in conversation for work situations, especially for business meetings and the like. Because many of them work all day, their classes might best be held in the evenings. Childcare could be important to them because both parents may want to attend the class.

Another church is located in an area with many Chinese, Vietnamese, and Filipino blue-collar workers. Many of them do shift work, which makes them unavailable for regular class hours during the week. Also, most of them share childcare with a spouse. One spouse takes the child during one work shift while the other parent takes the child during another shift. These learners are often tired and couldn't face a class during the week, especially in the evenings. Weekend classes might be better for them.

Another church is surrounded by Hispanic migrant workers who do seasonal work. When a particular crop is in, they work long hours and are unable to attend English classes. They need a class schedule that is flexible with the up-and-down swings of their work.

Still others churches may be in areas where there are many elderly immigrants or stay-at-home mothers who would like to get out of the house during the daytime. They might want classes during the morning hours of each weekday to see their friends and learn a little English. They may want socializing as much as learning English. Conversation groups and field trips might work well with these groups.

Finally, another church is near a couple of local colleges. Here young university students or business people might be looking for English tutoring to help them in their college subjects. They probably have odd schedules as they try to juggle classes and jobs. Perhaps individual tutoring or a lab setting would suit these individuals.

All of these examples show that each community is different. Each individual is different.

As you can see, you can customize your program according to time of day, type of program, childcare, social activities, and the like. In chapter 1 I talked about customizing in terms of letting learners choose what kind of assistance they want from the church. Chapter 6 discusses customizing in terms of allowing learners to choose the type of materials they want to study.

But customizing isn't just for the learners. You get choices too! What will work best for your church? Don't feel forced to choose something you know won't work. Sometimes it may feel like a tug-of-war as you try to balance the needs of your learners with the needs of your congregation, but generally speaking, the interests of both parties can be well served!

I've spent a great deal of time in this book discussing how to customize an ESL program at every level, from the assessment to the evaluation procedures. By following my suggestions, you will be creating a customized ESL program on your church campus. To take the guesswork out, I have attempted to supply you with most of the resources that you'll need.

There is one subject that I still haven't discussed—how you can customize your church and its services to better meet the needs of the ESL learner. Perhaps this suggestion makes some of you uncomfortable. You might be wondering if I'm suggesting that local congregations make a major overhaul of their structures and traditions to cater to the needs of ESL learners. You may be thinking, Why should we have to change what we're doing at our church? These people should be learning our ways. If this is a sore spot, you're not alone. I have encountered these feelings in a number of churches and denominations.

Perhaps some of you feel just the opposite. You're saying, We're ready! What should we do? How can we change our church to be more accommodating for these individuals? We want to include these people from our community in our church.

Jesus did tell us to "Go and make disciples of all nations . . . " (Matt. 28:19-20). And in many communities, those nations happen to be at our back door. You don't have to go to

Timbuktu to share the good news of Jesus. It can happen in your local church, two blocks from your house.

There may be people in your church who object to having "too many foreigners." These people are afraid of losing control, of losing what they have. They're not sure what this scenario—opening their doors to ESL learners—is going to look like. In fact, the immigrants I have observed in church settings have no desire to take over the church. Most are thrilled and grateful that people are willing take the time to get to know them and share the resources of the church with them. They often look for ways to express their appreciation—cooking, buying gifts, and the like.

We must rid ourselves of "us" and "them" thinking. If we are afraid of individuals coming into the church and sucking up resources or changing things, let's make realistic plans for how to deal with that. Let's ask for the Lord's provision. Remember, we serve a God who turned a couple of loaves and fish into a banquet. We don't need to be afraid of sharing with others because we can trust God to meet our church's needs.

Let me share a personal perspective. When I was employed as an ESL consultant in the private sector, I was often called in to help learners in picking up the corporate culture of an individual business. I was often given large, cumbersome training manuals, which I was to convert into ESL materials, so that employees could learn specific information related to their jobs. Employees also attended company-led training classes but sometimes had minimal success in understanding the materials presented. It was my job to assess why this was so. When I attended the classes myself and viewed the course materials through ESL learners' eyes, it was obvious to me why they could not absorb the information.

The courses were full of jargon, slang, and idioms. Specific skills were assumed—the ability to listen to a lecture, take notes and pick out the main points, ask for clarification, make requests, agree or disagree, and offer suggestions.

In addition to the language difficulties, there were cultural difficulties. For example, managers would often complain to me that it was like pulling teeth to get their employees to verbally take part in weekly meetings. The problem was that many of the ESL learners didn't know the company rules. They didn't know if it was okay for them to give their opinion to their boss, even if he or she specifically asked them what they thought. I was dealing with many Asian learners who believed it was wrong to express disagreement because they were taught that the boss is always right. The boss was a parent figure to whom you showed the greatest respect by keeping quiet and by listening.

What does all of this have to do with the church? Whether we realize it or not, we have cumbersome church manuals (hymnals and Bibles). We have unspoken expectations about the skills that people need to have to attend church school—for example, small group discussion skills. Church services are full of Christian jargon. Sermons are filled with slang, idioms, and high-level vocabulary. We have "rules" about appropriate behavior, such as what kind of clothes to wear, when to keep silence, when to stand up or sit down.

Please understand that I am not trying to pick on churches! All these are normal cultural expressions that have developed throughout the centuries. I'm simply saying that we need to begin to develop cultural sensitivity and an awareness of how the church looks to the outsider, especially to the ESL learner. I am not suggesting that churches push aside everything they do, but perhaps they could offer a little assistance to newcomers.

Some of you still might be thinking, Why should our church be making these changes anyway? Don't these people have their own church services to attend? It is true that many congregations serve individuals who speak a particular language. But what about the people who would like to get involved at a church that is close to their house, and your church happens to be it? What about immigrants who don't want to associate only with others from their own country? What about those who want to be part of a multiethnic congregation? I have heard these views often expressed by the learners I come in contact with.

The issue here is accessibility. Our churches should be as accessible to those of a different ethnic background as they are to those who are disabled. A good friend of mine put it best: We're just sliding over to make a little extra room at the dinner table for one more person.

But how do we go about beginning to put these attitudes into practice in real life? Here are a few suggestions. At our church we're still experimenting in this area, so this is by no means a complete list of what could be done. It's only a beginning.

1. **Invite ESL learners to church services and activities.**

   I'm serious. If you don't invite them, they probably won't come. From our evaluations we know that learners often don't come to church activities because they think that they're not allowed to attend since they are not Christians. (They want to come though. They're curious!)

2. **Give tours of the church.**

   If I went to a Buddhist temple, I would want a tour. ESL learners who aren't familiar with your church and/or your religion feel the same way. Show them around the church campus and explain what activities happen in different areas. I showed learners the Cry Room, our soundproof room for mothers who want to participate in the church service without their child making a disturbance for others. One Asian man commented, "How nice! You have a room for people to be sad in!"

3. **Let learners observe normal church activities and ask questions.**

   On occasion, we have taken fifteen minutes out of our normal Sunday classes to walk to the sanctuary and sit in the balcony to watch baptisms, communion services, child dedications, special music, drama, and the like. When we go back to class, learners have an opportunity to ask questions about what they saw. There is no pressure for them to participate in the service, yet they can have their curiosity assuaged about what Christians do in that building for an hour every Sunday.

4. **Make announcements about upcoming activities.**

   Each week, I look at church bulletins and newsletters to determine if there are activities that might interest ESL learners. I put these on a bulletin board.

5. **Work with church leaders to get materials for upcoming events and prepare learners in advance for the activity.**

   This takes a little doing, but it works! I have obtained the music scores and drama scripts from concerts and plays offered at our church prior to the actual event. I have also gotten cassette tapes of the music and given them to my learners so that they can begin learning the music beforehand. Learners really liked this because they could attend the event and understand it just like everyone else.

I also hope to begin working with my pastors to obtain sermon materials in advance. Then perhaps high-intermediate/advanced learners could attend an adjunct class at 9:00 a.m. on Sunday mornings that covers the sermon topic. Learners could do exercises that focus on the listening skills and vocabulary required to understand the sermon. Then they could attend our 10:45 a.m. worship service and be more prepared to understand the materials being presented. Sounds like a lot of work and cooperative effort, doesn't It? It's all about teamwork.

6. **Use the buddy system for classes, church services, activities, joining ministries, and the like.**

Learners are often afraid to try things in the church because they don't know the rules. I have seen ESL learners participate in activities with another member of the church that I know they never would have tried on their own. Some of our learners have sung in our choir. I went with them at first, and other choir members soon took them under their wings. We sit with learners during church services and help them through the order of worship. We take notepads and write summary notes to help them understand what the pastor is talking about. We help them with the homework from various classes offered at the church. At the annual women's retreat we act as buddies to the ESL women all weekend and have rooms next to theirs. Many other people in the church can do these things as well.

7. **Make a worship music tape.**

We are in the process of making a cassette tape of songs and accompanying lyrics that we normally sing in our worship service. Learners can listen to it in class and at home and learn the songs in order to participate more fully in the worship service.

8. **Offer activities that encourage members and learners to meet.**

The ESL church school class could meet with another adult class and interview each other about some topic. One thing I do is to send learners out on the patio between services and have them speak with church members while they drink coffee together. Another activity could be to have a game night or a cooking night. Our church has a newcomer's lunch in which people new to the church can meet the church staff and ask questions in an informal setting. ESL learners attend this lunch and meet members of the church.

9. **Meet with leaders in your church— deacons, secretaries, childcare workers.**

Leaders need to be informed how they can best work with ESL learners. Make language and intercultural information available to these individuals. (See Tips for Deacons in chapter 4 for examples.)

10. **Show learners how to use church systems.**

Give them pamphlets from the information booth. Show them how to bring their children to the nursery. Talk them through the phone call that they will have to make to register for a class.

11. **Get learners on your church mailing list.**

    Keep them informed about what is happening on your campus.

12. **Ask learners to do small jobs.**

    Several of our learners have acted as greeters on Sunday mornings for worship services. A few of them help me set up and tear down equipment for class. A couple of others have become our unofficial party coordinators for ESL class activities. Sometimes our advanced learners help out with the beginning ESL class, or they give their testimony to the seekers' groups. Some learners have done gardening on the church grounds. Others have run games or served food at our Fall Family Festival. One learner is now a teacher's aide for a children's church school class. Two of our new Christians worked in the church hospitality booth greeting first-time visitors to the church. We especially encourage our new believers to get involved in ministry projects when possible.

13. **Offer special services when needed.**

    Recently, we held a dedication service for the child of an Asian man who was leaving the U.S. on business for a year or more. This was unusual because the service did not occur when all of the other dedications for the church were scheduled. We held a special service just for him. The point is to be flexible.

    Our ESL new Christian believers who joined the church wanted to study the Bible more than just in a church service. Many were too nervous to attend a scheduled Bible study at the church, and/or their work schedules did not mesh with the class time. A member of our congregation decided to meet with some of those learners to study the Bible. We currently have two ESL believers' groups going; these individuals can meet at a time of their choice and work at a pace they are comfortable with.

14. **Let learners know about ongoing ministries and annual events that they can participate in.**

    The following (pg. 79) is a handout that learners receive when they enter the ESL program; it lets them know what we want and encourages them to get involved in the church.

At the heart of a customized program is flexibility and service, not only for those who are running the program but also for the members of the congregation. It's a team effort! Sometimes it takes a bit of time to develop these attitudes. Give it the time it takes. If the members in your church are moving slower, please be patient and pray! It might take members some time to catch the vision for an ESL program at your church. You may have to go it alone for a while. Often, members have to see the program in action before they can really understand it and get behind it. I must regularly remind myself that God is in control of what happens on our church campus. If God wants something to happen, it will happen!

ESL Students . . .

Here's How You Can Help at the Church!

1. **Gardening** (help with gardening around the church)

2. **Greeter** (say good morning to people as they come into church)

3. **Usher** (give people a bulletin and help them find a seat in the church)

4. **Teacher's Aide for Church School or Bible School** (help a teacher teach the children)

5. **Nursery Helper** (take care of the small children and babies one time a month)

6. **Fall Family Festival Worker** (set-up, clean-up, games, food)

7. **Helping Others** (cook a meal, clean a house)

8. **Women's Retreat** (decorate, set up or clean up for activity like tea or dancing)

9. **Christmas Musical** (help with lights and sound, painting sets, singing, dancing, making costumes)

10. **Greeter at Living Nativity** (say hello to new people at the church)

11. **Easter** (help with set-up and clean-up for egg hunt)

12. **Prayer Ministry** (pray for people)

13. **Giving** (food, money, or time to help the homeless)

You're Invited!

Church Activities for ESL Students

1. Sweetheart Dinner (Valentine's Day), *February*

2. Couple's Retreat, *February*

3. Men's Retreat, *March*

4. Easter Church Service, *March/April*

5. Easter Egg Hunt, *March/April*

6. Fourth of July Church Service, *July*

7. Church Picnic, *August*

8. Family Camp, *June-August*

9. Women's Retreat, *September*

10. Fall Family Festival, *October*

11. Thanksgiving Church Service, *November*

12. Living Nativity, *December*

13. Christmas Musical, *December*

14. Christmas Eve Church Service, *December*

15. Special Music Concerts, *All Year, to be announced*

16. Newcomer's Lunch, *Four times a year*

CHAPTER 9

Model Programs

Learning can be structured in several ways. The most common structure is the traditional classroom setting: a teacher standing in the front of the room and a group of students (and sometimes their tutors) sitting at tables facing him or her. Many ESL programs I have visited use this format, and it seems to work well. We always seem to start out with the format that seems most comfortable to us.

But there are also other formats that can be used in ESL instruction. Small groups work well for conversation and pronunciation. One-on-one tutoring has been used successfully for all English skills (but it's not ideal for conversation if you want to have more than two peoples' points of view represented in the discussion).

Traditional classroom settings seem to work best if you have a number of learners who are at approximately the same English level and who are willing to work on the same skills. The problem you'll encounter if you put out a general advertisement offering ESL at your church is that learners of different backgrounds and needs will come walking through your door. You'll probably have an advanced learner who wants to study for a college entrance exam, a beginner who can barely say hello and goodbye, and people whose skills are everywhere in between! What can you do?

Some churches have attempted to group learners of differing levels into one class and teach them together. These multilevel classes can be extremely difficult to teach, even for the trained ESL instructor. Trying to keep learners happy in a class like that is . . . well, difficult, to say the least! Putting adult-

beginner language learners together in a class with adult-advanced language learners is like putting a first-grade child with a sixth-grade child and expecting them to study the same curriculum. It can make instructors go a little crazy!

I'm not saying you can't have a multilevel class, but I strongly recommend that the levels be limited. For example, you could create a beginner class (levels 1 and 2) or an intermediate class (levels 3 and 4) or an advanced class (levels 5 and 6). This arrangement will contribute greatly to your sanity and to your learners' happiness. But what if you don't get enough individuals to make up a class? And even if you are lucky enough to get learners all from the same English level, what if they don't want to study the same skill?

At our church we are using a combination of learning structures. For our Christian ESL course we use traditional-level classes: a beginning and an intermediate class with some small group activities. As learners become Christians, we move them into small group structures so that they can receive more care and discipleship than a traditional classroom setting offers.

For the group using secular materials we use a language laboratory model that incorporates individual tutoring and small group activities. Which learning structures you use will be a recipe that only you can create. Start with what you're comfortable doing and then experiment as you progress.

The Lab Model

Because of the difficulty of teaching multilevel classes, I propose an alternate language teaching model, in which learners at a variety of levels can study a number of different skills of their own choosing. Also, instead of using individual tutoring (the tutor and the learner meet together off-site), tutors and learners are all in one location and are able to share with each other about what works and what doesn't. This goes a long way in preventing tutor burnout.

Another advantage of this model is that tutors can be tutors, not teachers. Learners understand that they are studying with volunteers—they don't expect the tutor to be God because he or she is standing in the front of the classroom.

Lab hours can be flexible according to your tutors' and learners' wishes. For example, after you have your lab up and running with set hours, you could expand those hours based upon the availability of the tutors. One tutor may be available from 10:00 a.m. to 12:00 p.m., and another from 11:00 a.m. to 1: 00 p.m. Thus, depending on the number of learners you have, the lab could be open from 10:00 a.m. to 1:00 p.m., and tutors could still maintain their individual schedules. The same is true for learners— they can't always come and go at exactly the time you want them to. A lab allows flexibility. Think of it as an open house in which people can come and go as needed.

The only difficulty with this kind of flexible system is making sure you always have a couple of tutors assigned to the lab on a particular day. That takes communication on the part of the tutors and the coordinators. To formalize it, you could have each tutor write down her schedule and optimum hours and then work up a schedule based upon everyone's availability.

Don't forget to plan with the learners' schedules in mind too. I let the learners at our program pick the lab hours. They chose the day of the week, time of day, and

number of hours they thought it should be open, based on how much they wanted to study. If we get enough requests for different hours, we do our best to accommodate them. Some learners come to the lab every week. Some don't. Some tutors come to the lab almost every week. Some don't. If we are flexible with our learners and our tutors without being judgmental, they will stick with us. You will just need one or two individuals who can be committed to the process on a weekly, ongoing basis so that there is some continuity for everyone involved.

What Does a Lab Look Like?

Learning labs can be exciting places because there is so much potential in the types of activities you could have. The room could be divided into different areas:

- A check-in area containing a desk, file cabinet, and bookshelves. Learners can check in, check out, check out books, sign up for help with a tutor, and get information.
- A testing area that is relatively quiet and secure (to prevent cheating), containing a table and chairs, timers, pencils, and index cards with numbers on them for waiting if there is a long line. (Files with testing guidelines, scoring procedures, and initial placement tests should be stored in a file cabinet by the check-in desk for security reasons.)
- A computer area; a listening area with tape recorders, CD ROM, and Dictaphones; a TV viewing area for work with videotapes or caption machine.
- Activity areas for small pronunciation and conversation groups (with chairs in a semicircle); a kitchen area for cooking lessons and parties.

- Work areas with tables and chairs for individual study or with a tutor.

These are just some of the possibilities. At our church we are experimenting right now, so we haven't come up with all the permutations. Find out what your learners would like!

How Many Tutors Should a Lab Have?

That depends. How many learners do you have? How many people from your church volunteer to be tutors? Ideally, if you have about thirty learners, it would be good to have six volunteer tutors scheduled at any one time. Unfortunately, this is not always possible. The absolute minimum number of tutors that can run a lab of thirty individuals is two people. Obviously, learners aren't going to get as much assistance as they would like in this scenario, but you have to be realistic and work with the number of available tutors.

If you have only two tutors working, one person must remain at the desk to check people and materials in and out and answer questions. That person can also tutor learners while seated at the desk when she has time. The other tutor circulates among the learners, answering questions. Generally speaking, learners will sign up to see a tutor at the desk. A tutor will work with each person on the list for twenty minutes and then move onto the next learner. If time permits, the tutor can go back and work with the same learner again. If there are many tutors, then all the tutors should work off the same list, crossing each name off after they have worked with the individual.

What Are Some Potential Problems with a Lab Setting?

The first problem that I foresee is materials disappearing. You will need to have a secure area (a locked cupboard or room) to make sure learners and/or members of your congregation don't borrow items. Also, you will need to follow the materials check-out policy I have described, or else come up with one of your own.

The second potential problem is that of financing the lab. We have received materials in a number of ways. Teachers have donated some books. Learners have donated their old textbooks. Church members have donated their older computers and software. Some church members have donated money to buy equipment. The church itself has allocated a budgeted amount to buy books and equipment. We keep one or two copies of a text in the lab. Learners can look at them and then order and pay for the books that they want to use. We have a variety of books so that learners don't have to purchase everything they would like to try.

A third problem is that of having low-beginning learners in the lab. Some beginners can work independently using textbooks, and some cannot. You may need to form a small group of beginners within the lab who are attended to by one specific tutor. This group could meet in one corner of the lab and work on the same materials together each week.

Here are a few tips for training volunteer tutors in how to run the lab.

- Discuss the concept of a lab and why you have chosen this format as opposed to a traditional classroom setting.
- Explain each area of the lab to the tutors and go over all of the procedures.
- Give tutors time to familiarize themselves with some of the ESL texts on the bookshelves.
- Be sure to go over the necessary forms used in the lab, including publisher order forms.

- Do several dry runs using role-play. Let tutors practice the various procedures on each other.
- When the lab opens, make sure tutors have a copy of the procedures. Have tutors carry them around as they begin working with learners so that they don't forget anything!

ESL Lab Procedures

Procedures for First-Time Attenders

1. Tutor, introduce yourself and welcome the person.

2. Ask if the person wants to study materials from the lab or to bring in his own materials to study. If he wants to use lab materials, give him the Continuing Student Profile. If he wants to study his own materials, give him the Walk-In Student Profile. If he seems like a beginner and it appears that he can't fill out the form, assume that he is a continuing student and sit down to help him fill out the form when you do steps 4-11. Otherwise ask him to sit down and fill out the form himself.

3. Get a copy of these procedures for you to follow, a folder, a stapler, file-folder label, a pen, and a Daily Progress Record, and then join the learner at his table.

4. Staple a Daily Progress Record inside a file folder on the left side. Put on a label at the top of the folder and write the learner's last name first and then his first name (e.g., Nguyen, Dai). Make sure you ask the learner if you don't know which name is which!

5. Help the learner finish the profile form if he has any questions and then look it over to make sure it is complete. Talk with your learner and make sure you know what he wants to study. Write it

in his folder on the first line under "activity." Keep the profile form in the learner's folder so that any tutor can pick it up and have some basic information about the learner.

6. Explain to the learner that later he will take a short test, and then he will be able to choose some materials to study with your help. Tell him that he can try different materials if he would like.

7. Explain the daily check-in procedures, including picking up a folder, checking out materials, and signing up to see a tutor.

8. Explain the need for and the procedures for ordering materials.

9. Ask the learner if she has any questions. Show her your name tag and point to the desk where she can come up and ask questions at any time.

10. Sign your initials, date it, and write "start up" in the activity section on the learner's Daily Progress Report. (This will help you make sure that each learner received his initial instructions.)

11. Ask the learner if he has time for testing today. If so and time permits, take him to the testing area.

12. Administer the test, grade it, and assign him a level. Write his test scores in his folder.

Testing

1. Take the written cloze test, oral interview, test grading guidelines, timer, and learner's folder out of the file.

2. Give the learner a pencil.

3. Take him or her to the testing area.

4. Explain that you will give a short, two-part test for speaking and writing. Tell the learner that he should try to relax because there are no right or wrong answers. These tests help us to determine his English level and what materials will be right for him. Give the cloze test first. (Follow the directions on the guidelines sheet.)

5. Give the oral interview second. (Follow the directions on the guidelines sheet.)

6. Be sure to watch that the learner does not copy work or talk to other learners during the testing period.

7. Collect the test and pencil at the end of the test. If time permits, correct the test, following the grading guidelines, and write the learner's oral score, written score, and appropriate level in the learner's folder on the Daily Progress Record sheet on the level line. Put your initials next to the scores. If the learner is a beginning student, put a blue-dot sticker on the top portion of his folder next to his name. That will alert any tutor that this learner is a beginner and requires additional outside assistance whenever he comes into the lab.

Note: If there are several learners waiting to be tested, you can give the cloze test to a few people at the same time, especially if this will free up another tutor to do oral interviews. Just follow the same procedures, especially number 6.

If there are many people waiting for an interview, make sure that you call the learners up in numerical order by using index cards with numbers on them.

Ordering Books

1. After testing, the learner will need to choose the materials that she wants to study. Look at her folder and profile form to determine what language skills she wants to learn. Show her the list of books currently available at the lab that are at her English level and of interest to her.

2. Let the learner examine a copy of the materials at her level from the bookshelf to see if she likes them. You can let her try them for a short time in the lab if she can't decide.

3. If the learner likes the text, help her look it up in the appropriate catalog. Then help her to fill out the order form.

4. Explain that she must send in the form with a check or money order or call or fax the publisher with her credit card number.

5. Explain to the learner that she can check out the book from the lab until her copy arrives in the mail.

   Note: ESL program coordinators should always be on the lookout for new materials that learners can try out in the lab.

Procedures for Regularly Attending Tutors

1. Starting on the second day and thereafter, a learner picks up his folder at the check-in desk and tells the tutor what materials he'll be working on.

2. The learner signs up for help with the tutor if needed on the Daily Tutor Sign-Up sheet.

3. Tutors sign up beginners immediately on the Daily Tutor Sign-Up sheet to

make sure someone is checking in on them each time they're in the lab.

4. Learners check out materials and equipment.

5. Tutors write in time, date, and learner's activity in the folder.

6. A learner can change borrowed materials after everyone has checked out materials for the first time.

7. When finished, learners turn in borrowed materials and folder to desk and check out.

Materials/Equipment Checkout

1. Before checking them out, a learner examines books belonging to the lab only at the check-out desk with a tutor.

2. If the learner wants to check out a book or equipment, he writes the book title or name of the equipment in his folder.

3. The tutor initials it.

4. The learner gives his driver's license or I.D. to the tutor.

5. The tutor files the license number under the last name in the materials check-out box (index-file card box with alphabetical spacers).

6. The tutor gives the learner materials or equipment.

7. When the learner returns materials, the tutor initials the folder and gives back the I.D.

Normal Duties of Tutors

1. Greet learners.

2. Get folders for learners.

3. Help learners check out materials.

4. Give tests to learners.

5. Grade tests for learners.

6. Tutor learners.

7. Familiarize self with books, materials, and equipment during slow times.

8. File folders alphabetically when learners check out materials.

9. Refile any used books, equipment, tapes, etc.

10. Communicate with and help other tutors.

11. Make announcements to learners about upcoming church events!

12. Make friends with learners—for example, go out for lunch with them if you have the time.

13. Pray for learners.

Forms

On the following pages, you'll find some of the forms and suggested equipment/ procedures that we use in the lab.

Walk-In Student Profile

Name_____
first   middle   last

Address_____
street   apt. #

City _____ State _____ Zip code _____

Telephone Number (_____) _____

Native Country _____ Native Language _____

1. Did you bring your own study materials today? What are they? (Please check one.)

  _____ materials from a college class

  _____ materials from work

  _____ materials from adult school or other training school

  _____ something from home (a bill; papers you want explained)

  _____ the newspaper

  _____ a letter (one that you want to write; one from your child's teacher, etc.)

  _____ other (please explain) _____

2. How did you hear about our English lab? (Please check one.)

  _____ newspaper

  _____ my friends told me

  _____ I saw a sign (where?) _____

  _____ radio

  _____ brochure (where?) _____

Continuing Student Profile

Name _____
       first   middle   last

Address _____
        street   apt. #

City _____ State _____ Zip code _____

Telephone Number (_____) _____

Native Country _____ Native Language _____

(Please check one.) _____ male _____ female

1.   Length of time in this country. _____

2.   Reason for coming to this country. _____

3.   What do you do during the daytime?
     _____ Student

     _____ Homemaker

     _____ Job outside of home (Please explain.) _____

     _____ Retired

     _____ Other (Please explain.) _____

4.   Reason for coming to the lab. (Please check one or more.)
     _____ I need more English to get a job.

     _____ I need more English to speak or write better at my job.

     _____ I want to make friends with Americans/Canadians (native speakers of English).

     _____ I want to speak better English so I can help my children in school.

     _____ I want to get around the community better (shopping, post office, etc.).

     _____ I want to study in a college or university in the future.

_____ I need help with my homework from school.

_____ I just want to improve my English skills in general.

_____ Other. (Please explain.) _____

5. What skills are you most interested in working on? (Write 1 and 2 in the blank with 1 being your first choice.)

_____ Reading

_____ Vocabulary (learning new words)

_____ Writing

_____ Grammar

_____ Listening

_____ Speaking

_____ Pronunciation

_____ Life skills (how to get around the community, etc.)

6. What 3 subjects are you most interested in studying about? (Write 1, 2, and 3 in the blanks with 1 being the subject that you want to study the most.)

_____ Food (reading labels, finding items in store, ordering in a restaurant)

_____ Clothing (washing instructions, describing problems with clothing)

_____ Housing (finding an apartment, reporting problems to owner)

_____ Money (counting, getting change, opening checking/savings account)

_____ Calendar (days of the week, months, seasons)

_____ Post office (buying stamps, sending packages, money orders)

_____ Shopping (finding good deals, making returns, catalog shopping)

_____ Health (illnesses, reading medicine labels, making doctor appointments, current health issues)

_____ Jobs (job advertisements, applications, resumes, cover letters, interview skills, employer expectations)

_____ Schools (speaking to your child's teacher, colleges and universities)

_____ Cars (driving rules, signs, maintenance, license, registration, smog test)

_____ Insurance (different kinds, application forms)

_____ Holidays and North American culture (North American traditions, weddings, funerals)

_____ Government (President, Vice-president, Senate, House of Representatives)

_____ Recreation (where to go, getting information, making reservations, travel agents)

_____ Current events (reading newspapers, discussing the news)

_____ TOEFL (prepare for the TOEFL examination)

7. Do you need daycare when you're at the lab? _____ yes _____ no

8. Number of children? _____ ages? _____

9. How did you hear about our English lab? (Please check one.)

_____ Newspaper

_____ My friends told me

_____ I saw a sign (where?) _____

_____ Radio

_____ Brochure (where?)_____

CHAPTER 10

Additional Resources

Room Set-up Duties for Traditional Classroom or Small Groups in Lab

1. Turn on lights.

2. Open shades and curtains.

3. Open windows and doors or turn on air conditioning.

4. Set up whiteboards or chalkboards. Get pens, chalk, and erasers.

5. Set up chairs in a circle (or at tables, depending on your situation).

6. Set up cassette player for music.

7. Turn on TV and VCR. Get video ready.

8. Set up overhead and screen, and get pens.

9. Set out file box (containing extra pens, pencils, scratch paper, song sheets, initial placement tests, name tags, etc.).

10. Check coffeepot for water; set out refreshments.

11. Set out nametags, pens, clipboard with attendance roster.

12. Set up musical keyboard for singing (if applicable).

Flyer

On the following pages are a couple of the flyers that we placed in the community to advertise the language lab as well as our Sunday morning classes. The first one is pretty simple, but learners told me to keep it that way. We also have a newspaper ad that looks good because we used the same desktop publisher that the church uses to advertise. We're still developing a brochure, but in the meantime we had business cards printed, which we pass out to prospective new learners.

Free English Classes!

Beginning, Intermediate, and Advanced

Work on Your English Skills:

Conversation, Pronunciation, Listening, Reading, & Writing

Fun Activities:

Music, Games, Videos, Interviews, Parties,
Make Friends with Native English Speakers

Registration:

Classes Open Now!

Cost:

Free! You pay for books only.

Time:

Saturday Morning 10:00 a.m.-12:00 p.m.
Sunday Morning 10:30 a.m.-12:00 p.m.

Room:

E-201 (Go to the information center in the main building,
and someone will show you where it is.)

Childcare: Free!

(Sunday mornings only.)

We Hope You'll Come!

If you have any questions, please call (408) 262-8000 x 155.

**First Presbyterian Church of Milpitas
1435 Clear Lake at South Park Victoria
Milpitas, CA 95035**

(we put a map on the bottom)

Attention English as a Second Language Learners!!!

Are you not learning English because . . .

— you tried to get into an Adult School or Community College ESL class, but all the classes were closed?

— you are too busy during the week with work or school to go to an English class?

— you can't find a tutor to help you with your special English problems?

— ESL classes you have gone to in the past are boring?

— most ESL class times are not convenient for you?

— you don't want the stress of homework and tests?

If you answered YES to any of these questions, then maybe the English Language Center is the place for you!

We offer a variety of ways for you to improve your English in a friendly, comfortable environment!

— Visit our center and study reading, vocabulary, grammar, writing, listening, speaking, pronunciation, and TOEFL at all levels: beginning, intermediate, and advanced.

— Get help from a college ESL instructor and volunteer tutors.

— Progress at your own speed . . . you study materials as fast or as slow as you want.

— Participate in conversation and pronunciation groups.

— Use our computers, caption machine, and other equipment.

— Pay for only your materials.

— Convenient weekend hours.

— Open enrollment and registration.

— Center is open year-round.

— Sunday morning ESL classes with music, drama, games, videos, and more!

— Fun social activities: bowling, horseback riding, camping, golf, parties, concerts!

— Opportunities to get to know American people!

Does it sound good? Come in and see us, and we'll tell you more!

English Language Center
First Presbyterian Church of Milpitas
1435 Clear Lake at South Park Victoria
Milpitas, CA 95035
(408) 262-8000

Tutor Training Programs and Materials

1. **TESOL (Teachers of English to Speakers of Other Languages)**
700 S. Washington St., Suite 200
Alexandria, VA 22314
Tel. (703) 836-0774
Fax (703) 836-7864

   Be sure to sign up for the volunteer ESL tutor interest section—newsletters, journals, conventions, training, book exhibits—everything!

2. **CETC (Christian Educators in TESOL), a caucus of TESOL**
700 S. Washington St., Suite 200
Alexandria, VA 22314
Tel. (703) 836-0774
Fax (703) 836-7864

   Newsletter, meetings at TESOL conventions, the most complete Christian ESL materials list.

3. **Willow Creek Association**
P.O. Box 3188
Barrington, IL 60011-3188
Tel. (847) 765-0070 or (800) 570-9812
Fax (847) 765-5046

   Training seminars, books, and cassettes tapes available through the Church Leadership Conference or through the mail. Two courses I recommend are *Launching Seeker Small Groups* and *The Contagious Christian*. The first course teaches about how to start a small group for people who have no background in the Christian church. The groups are designed to help individuals in their journey towards faith in Christ. This style would work well with intermediate and advanced learners who want conversation on Christian topics. The latter course teaches individuals how to share their faith in a nonthreatening and sensitive manner.

(They also have a course on running a believers' small group.)

4. **North American Missions Board of the Southern Baptist Convention**
4200 North Point Parkway
Alpharetta, GA 30202-4176

   Ask for the *Literacy Missions Conversational English Workshop Manual*. Order from LifeWay Christian Resources, 1-800-448-8032.

5. **Catholic Charities**
Immigration, Refugee
and Youth Services
2625 Zanker Road, Suite 201
San Jose, CA 95134
Tel. (408) 944-0362 ext. 159

   Tutor training sessions, intercultural training for tutors, tutor-training materials.

6. **Beacon Hill Press of Kansas City**
P.O. Box 419527
Kansas City, MO 64141
Tel. 1-800-877-0100

   Wesley, Eby J. *Handbook for Teaching Bible-Based ESL* (1990). A complete discussion of the topic, including methodology, lesson planning resources, 143 pages.

7. **Joan M. Dungey**
126 North Walnut
Yellow Springs, OH 45387
Tel. (937) 767-7099

   Dungey, Joan M., and Carol Johnson. *Bible Studies for New English Speakers* (1986). A videotape produced by University Presbyterian Church, Seattle. Beginning and intermediate Bible ESL lessons are demonstrated; three-hour running time. Several experienced people demonstrate methods and give insights with panel discussions. Viewer's/leader's guide, thirty pages.

8. **World Relief /City Team Family Outreach**
USA Ministries
218 Kirk Avenue
San Jose, CA 95127
Tel. (408) 729-3786
Fax (408) 729-3086

Tutor-training materials, training sessions, curriculum list.

9. **Easy English**
100 Skyport Drive #206
San Jose, CA 95110-1374
Tel. (408) 453-6589

Tutor training.

10. **Audio/Video Forum**
Suite ESSAY
96 Broad Street
Guilford, CT 06437
Tel. 1-800-243-1234

Mcvey, William. *Practical ESL Teaching Techniques.* Four audiocassettes that present techniques for teaching essential ESL skills such as listening, speaking, pronunciation, reading, writing, vocabulary, and grammar.

11. **ESL Training Services**
212 West Brook Drive
Raleigh, NC 27615
Tel. (919) 847-3663

Reece, Glenda. *Conversational English Using the Lipson Method.* Videotape.

12. **All Nations Literature**
P.O. Box 26300
Colorado Springs, CO 80936-3600
Tel. 1-800-962-0080

Tutor-training video, Christian dictionary.

13. **Billy Graham Evangelistic Association**
P.O. Box 779
Minneapolis, MN 55440-0779

Training materials for sharing your faith and following up on new believers.

Secular ESL Publishers and Distributors

You can send for catalogs from all of these publishers and distributors.

1. **ALTA Book Center**
In Canada and U.S.A. (800) ALTA/ESL
In San Francisco, CA (415) 541-9470
(bookstore)
or
14 Adrian Court
Burlingame, CA 94010
Tel. (415) 692-1285
Fax (415) 692-4654 (distribution center, reading room)

2. **Prentice Hall Regents**
A Division of Simon & Schuster
One Lake Street
Upper Saddle River, NJ 07428
Tel. 1-800-922-0579

3. **Dominie Press, Inc.**
1949 Kellogg Ave.
Carlsbad, CA 92008
Tel. 1-800-232-4570

4. **Heinle & Heinle Publishers**
20 Park Plaza
Boston, MA 02116
Tel. 1-800-354-9706 or (877) 633-3375

5. **News for You**
New Readers Press
P.O. Box 35888, Department 20
Syracuse, NY 13235-5888
Tel. 1-800-448-8878

Intermediate level newspaper of current events.

6. **The University of Michigan Press**
   Baker and Taylor International Ltd.
   652 East Main Street
   Bridgewater, NJ 08807-0920
   Tel. (908) 707-0400
   Fax (908) 707-4387

7. **Jag Publications**
   11288 Ventura Boulevard #B-301
   Studio City, CA 91604

8. **Cambridge University Press**
   40 West 20th Street
   New York, NY 10011-4211
   Tel. 1-800-872-7423

9. **New Readers Press**
   Publishing Division of Laubach Literacy
   P.O. Box 35888
   Syracuse, NY 13235-5888

10. **Addison Wesley Longman**
    10 Bank St., Suite 900
    White Plains, NY 10606-1951

11. **Oxford University Press**
    198 Madison Avenue
    New York, NY 10016
    Tel. 1-800-451-7556

12. **Audio/Video Forum**
    Suite ESSAY
    96 Broad Street
    Guilford, CT 06437
    Tel. 1-800-243-1234

Christian ESL Publishers/Distributors

You can send for catalogs from all of these publishers and distributors.

1. **CRC Publications**
   2850 Kalamazoo Avenue SE
   Grand Rapids, MI 49560
   Tel. 1-800-333-8300
   Fax (616) 246-0834

   Literacy and ESL materials, tutor-resource list. (Ask for the Open Door Literacy Program Packet.)

2. **Multi-Language Media**
   P.O. Box 301
   Ephrata, PA 17522
   Tel. (717) 738-0582

   Bible Materials for ESL learners; Bible materials in other languages.

3. **American Bible Society**
   1865 Broadway
   New York, NY 10023
   Tel. 1-800-322-4253

4. **Honor Books**
   P.O. Box 55388
   Tulsa, OK 74155

5. **Beacon Hill Press of Kansas City**
   P.O. Box 419527
   Kansas City, MO 64141
   Tel. 1-800-877-0700

6. **Joan M. Dungey**
   126 North Walnut
   Yellow Springs, OH 45387
   Tel. (513) 767-7099

7. **Shepherd Ministries**
   2221 Walnut Hill Lane
   Irving, TX 75038-4410
   Tel. (972) 580-8000
   Fax (972) 580-1FAX

Testing Resources

1. **New Readers Press**
   P.O. Box 35888
   Syracuse, NY 13235-5888
   Tel. 1-800-448-8878
   Fax (315) 422-5561

   BEST Placement Tool, Form B or Form C. Achievement tests for listening, reading, writing, and conversation. These achievement tests can be used alone or as part of a complete life-skills program for beginning learners. A student book, teacher's book, audiotape, and training video about how to use all of the materials are available. If you want information on the whole program, ask for information on "Life Prints," levels 1, 2, and 3.

2. **Comprehensive Adult Student Assessment System (CASAS)**
   5151 Murphy Canyon Point
   San Diego, CA 92123-1339
   Tel. (858) 292-2900, 1-800-255-1036

   CASAS Placement Tests, Achievement Tests, and Exit Tests. CASAS tests are used by many adult educational programs to determine at what level of instruction a person needs to begin, his achievement process while in the program, and at what time he would be able to exit the program. The tests often focus on English survival skills—for example, what you would need to say at the post office or the bank, etc. CASAS provides training sessions on how to use their tests. Ask about training sessions in your area. Tell them you are interested in using the tests for adult ESL and ask them to send you their "Life Skill Competencies" list. (This list will give you an idea of what English skills adult learners need to have to communicate in our society and will help you plan your curriculum.)

Intercultural and Linguistic Readings

1. Condon, John C., and Fathi S. Yousef. *An Introduction to Intercultural Communication.* Macmillian Publishing Company, 1987.

2. Samovar, Larry A., and Richard E. Porter. *Intercultural Communication: A Reader.* Wadsworth Publishing Company, 1988.

3. Kraft, Charles H. *Communication Theory for Christian Witness.* La Mirada, CA: Biola University.

4. Mayers, Marvin K. *Christianity Confronts Culture.* Academie Books, Zondervan Publishing Company, 1987.

5. Grunlan, Stephen A., and Marvin K. Mayers. *Cultural Anthropology.* Academie Books, Zondervan Publishing Company, 1988.

6. Ellison, Craig W. "Addressing Felt Needs of Urban Dwellers." *Urban Mission,* March, 1987.

7. Nunan, David. *Designing Tasks for the Communicative Classroom.* Cambridge University Press, 1989. (Check with Alta for this one.)

Attendance Roster

Please sign your name and put an "x" under the correct week each time you come.

Last Name/First Name	Wk 1	Wk 2	Wk 3	Wk 4	Wk 5	Wk 6	Wk 7	Wk 8	Wk 9	Wk 10
1										
2										
3										
4										
5										
6										
7										
8										
9										
10										
11										
12										
13										
14										
15										
16										
17										
18										
19										
20										

Daily Progress Record

Name_____Level_____

Date	In Out	Book/Activity	Tutor

Daily Tutor Sign-Up

Today's Date_____

Name	Time	Book/Activity	Location

Equipment List for Lab

1. Television
2. VCR
3. Tape recorder(s)
4. CD player
5. CD ROM player (CDs)
6. Whiteboard, chalkboard, flip chart
7. Computers (software)
8. Camera
9. Video camera
10. Dictaphones
11. Caption machine
12. Textbooks
13. Games
14. Reference books
15. Coffee pot, cups, napkins, coffee, tea, etc.
16. Timer
17. File cabinet
18. Tables, chairs
19. Bookcase(s) or cabinet
20. Door locks
21. Shades or curtains
22. Clipboard and pen for Daily Tutor Sign-Up sheet
23. Baskets, file-folder organizers
24. File folders
25. File labels and black dot stickers
26. Staplers, pens, pencils
27. Computer paper, scratch paper
28. Index card file box, alphabetical spacers
29. Whiteboard pens, chalk, erasers

Lab Set-Up Duties

1. Turn on lights.
2. Open shades and curtains.
3. Open windows and doors or turn on air conditioning.
4. Set up whiteboard or chalkboard; get pens and erasers or chalk.
5. Set up chairs and/or tables.
6. Set up audio, TV, VCR.
7. Set up overhead and screen.
8. Check files to be sure they are organized.
9. Check coffeepot for water; set out refreshments, paper supplies.
10. Set out nametags, pens, attendance check-in roster.
11. Set up keyboard.
12. Turn on computers.

Printed in the United States
54927LVS00001B/133-302